**CFRE Exam Compass™
STUDY GUIDE**

2025 Edition

EDITED BY Paula J. Jenkins, CFRE; Jeff Stanger; Eva Aldrich, Ph.D., CAE, (CFRE, 2001-2016)
PUBLISHED BY CFRE International
225 Reinekers Lane, Suite 625, Alexandria, VA 22314, USA

www.CFRE.org
© 2025 CFRE International
All rights reserved. No portion of this book may be reproduced in any form without permission from the publisher, except as permitted by U.S. copyright law. For permissions contact:
Learn@CFRE.org
Cover by Cordy Gonzalez Art Direction & Design
Interior by Cordy Gonzalez Art Direction & Design
ISBN: 978-1-7347235-3-3

Table of Contents

Acknowledgments		3
Introduction		4
Section One:	Your CFRE Journey: Getting Started	7
Section Two:	Learning to Think Like a CFRE	14
Section Three:	Understanding the Knowledge Domains	20
Domain 1:	Current & Prospective Donor Research	20
Domain 2:	Securing the Gift	32
Domain 3:	Relationship Building	44
Domain 4:	Volunteer Involvement	54
Domain 5:	Leadership & Management	63
Domain 6:	Ethics, Accountability, and Professionalism	76
Section Four:	Test-Taking Strategies for the CFRE Exam	90
Section Five:	Preparing for and Taking the CFRE Exam	96
Section Six:	After the CFRE Exam	100
Section Seven:	Creating Your Personal Study Plan	102
Section Eight:	Congratulations! You're a CFRE. Now What?	105
Appendix I	Recommended Reading	107
Appendix II	Study Questions and Answers	110
Appendix III	Policy on Accountability Standards	116
Endnotes		119

ACKNOWLEDGMENTS

CFRE International would like to thank the following: Paula Jenkins for her role in making this study guide happen, the CFRE International Board of Directors for their support during the process, the CFRE International Exam Committee for their technical assistance, and finally, CFREs worldwide for their continued commitment to ethical fundraising.

INTRODUCTION

The Certified Fund Raising Executive (CFRE®) certification program raises professional standards in fundraising and designates individuals who possess the knowledge of best practices in ethical fundraising—best practices that are essential for sustaining nonprofit organizations and growing the philanthropic sector. Founded in 1981, the CFRE certification program has evolved to mirror the evolution of fundraising practices and professionalism.

This study guide is meant to assist candidates for CFRE certification in preparing for success on the CFRE exam, which is a comprehensive examination covering the wide range of fundraising best practice. Review the sections of the study guide sequentially to derive the most benefit from the study guide.

Using the Study Guide

The study guide outlines the key knowledge areas that qualified candidates need to know to be successful in taking the CFRE exam. The study guide starts with a review of the CFRE Test Content Outline and asks you to complete a self-assessment regarding your familiarity with exam content. As you complete the self-assessment, consider why a fundraising professional needs to have this knowledge.

The study guide also asks you to consider your learning style and how you can utilize your learning preferences as you prepare for the CFRE exam. Your way of preparing to take the CFRE exam may not be the same as the way other candidates prepare, and that is to be expected. What is important is for you to determine the study methods that are most effective for you.

The CFRE exam is designed to identify individuals who have the knowledge of best practices in ethical fundraising required for success as a fundraising professional. As you read through the study guide, you may find that some fundraising procedures at your organization differ from what is generally accepted best practice in fundraising. Remember that the CFRE exam tests your knowledge of best practices in ethical fundraising. It does not necessarily reflect how you may conduct fundraising activities on a day-to-day basis at your particular organization. This is an important point that deserves emphasis.

The study guide is just one tool you can use to help you prepare for the CFRE exam. Successful candidates typically spend at least 40 hours preparing for the CFRE exam and employ multiple methods as part of their preparation. Other methods of preparation that you may find helpful include taking the CFRE Practice Exam, reviewing books on the CFRE Resource Reading List, finding a local or online study group, and connecting with other candidates and mentors through the CFRE Central online community. You may also check with your professional association to see if they offer the CFRE Exam Compass™ preparation course, which is available exclusively from CFRE Participating Organizations.

Preparing for Success

For the best chance of success on the CFRE exam, begin studying early. Examine the CFRE Test Content Outline to determine areas where you might benefit from additional knowledge, and plan your professional development opportunities accordingly. Remember that most CFREs report having spent at least 40 hours on exam preparation.

If you need motivation to carve out study time, remember the reasons why you are pursuing CFRE certification. These may include:

- Self-satisfaction.
- Enhanced knowledge of fundraising best practices.
- Pride in the fundraising profession and in yourself as a fundraising professional.
- Career advancement—most CFREs report they hold upper management positions.[1]
- Greater earning potential—in 2018, the average salary earned by CFREs in the United States was over USD $20,000 more per year than their non-certified counterparts. The average salary earned by CFREs in Canada was nearly CAD$40,000 more per year than their non-certified counterparts.[2]

Once certified, CFREs report that the process of studying for the CFRE exam was beneficial and enjoyable! Approach your preparation with a positive attitude and take time to appreciate the learning process. Once completed, you will have a greater knowledge of fundraising best practices that will translate into increased success and satisfaction in your fundraising work.

CFRE International and the CFRE Certification Program

CFRE International is the independent certifying body responsible for all governance, policies, standards, and administration of the CFRE certification program.

The CFRE certification program stands proudly as the only accredited, globally recognized certification for fundraising professionals. The CFRE certification program was first accredited in the U.S. in 2009 by the National Commission for Certifying Agencies (NCCA). The CFRE certification program remained accredited by NCCA through 2017, when the ANSI National Accreditation Board (ANAB) accredited the CFRE certification program under the ANSI/ISO/IEC 17024 standard for certification of personnel. ANAB accreditation means that the CFRE certification program is accredited according to international standards. As such, the CFRE credential is the world's only internationally recognized, accredited certification for philanthropic fundraising professionals.

ANAB accreditation is the hallmark of a rigorous, high-quality certification program. ANAB accreditation confers independent, widely respected national and international validation of both the CFRE certification program and the credential.

Research shows that accredited certification programs are consistently preferred by employers because they drive quality and improve results.[3] Accreditation by ANAB also means that the CFRE credential's global significance is recognized by other worldwide accrediting bodies with which ANAB has established multilateral recognition agreements. These accrediting bodies include the United Kingdom Accreditation Service (UKAS), the Joint Accreditation System of Australia and New Zealand (JAS-ANZ), the Deutsche Akkreditierungsstelle GmbH (DAkkS), and many others which also have IOS/IEC/17024 accredited programs for certification of persons.

Please note that the CFRE Study Guide, the CFRE Exam Compass preparation course, and other resources mentioned in this volume are independent of the CFRE exam. Members of the CFRE International Exam Committee (who are solely responsible for CFRE exam content) and CFRE International staff members supporting the work of the Exam Committee do not advise on CFRE exam preparation materials.

Also, please note that CFRE International does not endorse specific CFRE exam preparation resources. The Study Aids section of the CFRE International website provides a starting point for resources that may be helpful and includes the CFRE Practice Exam, CFRE Reading Resource List, CFRE Test Content Outline, and links to videos and study group listings. No preparation course or resource is a prerequisite for earning CFRE certification. Also, please note that because a course or resource claiming to prepare individuals for the CFRE exam uses "CFRE" in its title does not mean that the offering has been reviewed or endorsed by CFRE International. As in everything, be an informed consumer when choosing your preparation tools.

For More Information and Assistance with Your Application

- Log on to CFRE International's website at **CFRE.org,** where you can start your CFRE application and find the CFRE Candidate Handbook, which has complete information about the CFRE certification process. Please note that you may log in and out of your application as many times as you wish. There is no cost to start your application. Payment is due when you have fulfilled all application requirements and are ready to submit your application for review.
- Email CFRE International certification staff at **succeed@cfre.org.**
- Call CFRE International certification staff at **+1 571 699 0601.**

CFRE Ambassadors

The CFRE Ambassador Program connects future CFREs with current CFREs who are serving as Ambassadors. CFRE Ambassadors are available to speak one-on-one with future CFREs about their CFRE journey, including:
- Which study tools they found useful.
- How they studied.
- How they talked to their employer about supporting their CFRE journey.
- The benefits being a CFRE has had on their career.

To be put in touch with a CFRE Ambassador, email **share@cfre.org** with your name, city, state/province, and country. We will work to connect you via email with an ambassador within five business days.

CFRE Central Online Community

Individuals who have started their CFRE application can join CFRE Central, CFRE International's online community. There, you can connect with other CFRE applicants to find individuals in your area who want to form study groups, as well as with CFREs who can share their insights from completing the CFRE certification process.

Section One

Your CFRE Journey: Getting Started

Introduction

The Certified Fund Raising Executive (CFRE) certification signifies your confidence, ethics, and professionalism in fundraising. Individuals who hold and maintain the CFRE credential are committed to excellence in best practices in ethical fundraising and to being leaders in the fundraising profession. When you earn your CFRE certification, you join a distinguished group of more than 8,000 fundraising professionals worldwide who are dedicated to continuing education and professional development and who, as a result, enjoy enhanced career opportunities and increased organizational impact.

As philanthropy and fundraising continue to grow, so does CFRE certification. Founded in 2001, CFRE International is an independent nonprofit organization, the sole mission of which is dedicated to setting standards in philanthropy through a valid and reliable certification process for fundraising professionals: the CFRE credential.

Between 1981 and 1996, two leading professional associations had their own separate certification programs. The Association for Healthcare Philanthropy offered the CAHP, and the Association of Fundraising Professionals, formerly the National Society of Fund Raising Executives (NSFRE), offered the CFRE. In 1997 for the betterment of the entire profession, those two organizations merged their programs to form the independent CFRE Professional Certification Board, now CFRE International.

Following the creation of CFRE International, other leading philanthropic associations and nonprofit organizations joined in support of the program as CFRE Participating Organizations. There are approximately 30 CFRE Participating Organizations worldwide, with representation on six continents. CFRE International ensures the CFRE certification program remains dynamic, relevant, and supportive of the growth of best practices in ethical fundraising and growth of public trust in the fundraising profession.

Certification vs. Certificate—What's the Difference?

The CFRE certification program is the only accredited, globally recognized certification for fundraising professionals. While they may sound similar, a certification and a certificate are not the same.

A certification assures the public and employers that an individual has a certain level of professional experience and maintains specific knowledge required of practitioners at a certain level of professional attainment. Certification is awarded by a third-party, standard-setting organization. It is an assessment process that indicates mastery of knowledge, which is usually assessed through an exam. In addition, certification has ongoing requirements (usually in the areas of professional education, performance, and practice) if an individual is to maintain the certification.

A certificate may be awarded by educational programs or other organizations offering continuing education. It is an educational process that indicates completion of a course or series of courses with a specific focus. It is a "snapshot" that demonstrates knowledge of course content at the end of a set period of time.

Because CFRE is a certification program, individuals must first meet application requirements for professional education, practice, performance, and fundraising ethics. Only after these requirements are met are individuals approved to take the CFRE exam. CFRE International confers CFRE certification to individuals who take and pass the CFRE exam. Individuals who become CFREs are required to recertify every three years, which means they must continue to meet requirements in the areas of professional education, practice, performance, and fundraising ethics. More information about CFRE initial certification and CFRE recertification is available at **CFRE.org**.

Reasons to Earn CFRE Certification

There are many reasons to earn CFRE certification. Identify the reasons that are most important to you and refer to those reasons often to keep you motivated throughout the CFRE certification process. Some reasons that CFREs frequently cite for earning CFRE certification include:

1. *Certification grants you more credibility.*
   CFRE certification serves as an impartial, third-party endorsement of your knowledge and experience against international standards in philanthropy. It adds to your credibility as a professional and sets you apart from other fundraisers.

2. *Certification can improve career opportunities and advancement.*
   CFRE certification can give you the "edge" when being considered for a promotion or other career opportunities. CFRE certification clearly identifies you as an employee who has demonstrated mastery of fundraising principles and techniques based on accepted best practices.

3. *Certification prepares you for greater on-the-job responsibilities.*
   CFRE certification is a clear indicator of your willingness to invest in your own professional development. Certified professionals are aware of the constantly changing environment around their profession and possess the desire to anticipate and respond to change.

4. *Certification improves skills and knowledge.*
   Typically, achieving CFRE certification requires training, studying, and "keeping up" with changes. CFRE certification showcases your individual mastery by confirming proficiency and knowledge in the field. CFRE certification also requires recertification every three years, ensuring you stay ahead of the curve in fundraising.

5. *Certification may provide for greater earnings potential*
   Many fundraising professionals who have become CFRE certificants experience salary and wage increases based on their certification status. Studies show that on average CFRE certificants earn significantly more than their non-certified counterparts. In addition, CFRE certificants are in demand internationally.

6. *Certification demonstrates your commitment to the fundraising profession.*
   Receiving CFRE certification shows your peers, supervisors, and donors your commitment to your chosen career and your ability to perform to set standards.

7. *Certification enhances the profession's image.*
   The CFRE certification program seeks to grow, promote, and develop certified professionals, who can stand "out in front" as role models and ethical fundraising professionals in the fundraising field.

8. *Certification reflects achievement.*
   CFRE certification is a reflection of personal achievement because the individual has displayed mastery of his or her field by meeting requirements and standards in fundraising.

9. *Certification builds self-esteem.*
   CFRE certification is a step toward defining yourself beyond a job description or academic degree while gaining a sense of personal satisfaction.

10. *Certification offers greater recognition from peers.*
    As a CFRE certificant, you can expect increased recognition from your peers for taking that extra step in your professional career.

What Are the Requirements to Earn CFRE Certification?

Individuals seeking CFRE certification must fulfill the following application requirements before being approved to take the CFRE exam:

EDUCATION: 80 points (must be within the past 5 years). Education includes continuing education on fundraising topics (including conference attendance), academic degrees, teaching/speaking on fundraising topics, authoring on fundraising topics, and service learning through volunteer experience. Points are awarded as follows:

- **Continuing education:** 1 point for each hour spent attending educational conference sessions or workshops. 2 points for each hour spent teaching educational conference sessions or workshops using previously developed material. 3 points for each hour spent teaching educational conference sessions or workshops using newly developed material.
- **Authoring:** 5 points per published article (500 words or more; self-published material is ineligible). 15 points per book chapter. 30 points per book.
- **Academic degrees:** 5 points for an Associate's degree. 10 points each for a Bachelor's, Master's, or Doctoral degree. For initial certification, all academic degrees may be counted, even if the degree was earned more than five years ago and is in a major unrelated to fundraising.
- **Service Learning:** 2 points per year for each ongoing volunteer leadership role. 1 point per year for each instance of general volunteer service (a maximum of 10 will be counted). Volunteer work must be separate from employment or contractual obligations with a given organization.

A maximum of 10 points of non-fundraising related continuing education may also be counted, provided that the non-fundraising related content develops skills that will help the individual become a more proficient fundraising professional. Sessions on general leadership skills, time management, etc., are examples of non-fundraising related content that might be applicable.

PROFESSIONAL PRACTICE: 36 points (must be within the past 5 years). 1 month of employment = 1 point. Only 1 month will be awarded for any given month regardless of the number of employers or clients.

Candidates for the CFRE credential must be or have been employed full-time as a professional member of a fundraising staff or as a fundraising consultant to nonprofit organizations; at least 50% of their job duties and responsibilities must consist of fundraising activities, resource development, and/or the management of fund development which results in generation of philanthropic support.

Candidates who are or have been employed half-time (defined by CFRE International as 50% FTE or greater) may also qualify, providing 100% of their job duties and responsibilities consist of fundraising activities, resource development, and/or the management of fund development which results in generation of philanthropic support.

Consultants must submit a client list for the time period claimed as a consultant.

For professionals with less than 5 years (60 points) of employment in fundraising, completion of an academic degree in fundraising and/or an intensive certificate program in fundraising is highly recommended.

PROFESSIONAL PERFORMANCE: 55 points (must be within the past 5 years). Candidates can earn points in any of the following three areas, or a combination thereof. It is not necessary to document points in each of the categories.

- **Actual funds raised:** 1 point = Equivalent raised in candidate's local currency of USD $25,000. Fundraising professionals in non-OECD member countries will receive 1 additional point for each point of Actual Funds Raised.
- **Communications projects:** 5 points for each project with outcomes that had a measurable impact on the success of fundraising for the organization.
- **Management projects:** 5 points for each project with outcomes that had a measurable impact on the success of fundraising for the organization.

Examples of Communications and Management projects are available at **CFRE.org.**

Upon fulfillment of these requirements and application approval, individuals have one year in which to take the CFRE exam. More information about the CFRE initial application process is available on CFRE International's website.

Your Self-Assessment: Are You Ready to Earn CFRE Certification?

The CFRE Test Content Outline is based on research conducted by CFRE International regarding the work that fundraising professionals do on a regular basis as part of their job responsibilities in fundraising. Specifically, this research is called a job task analysis and is an important part of ensuring the validity of the test content outline for accredited certification programs. The CFRE Job Task Analysis surveys thousands of fundraising professionals around the globe at least every five years to identify:

- The tasks fundraising professionals perform.
- How often fundraising professionals perform those tasks.
- The importance of the tasks to fundraising success.
- The knowledge fundraising professionals use to perform the tasks.

A fundraising professional who has met the eligibility requirements to take the CFRE exam should have the knowledge needed to take and pass the exam. However, CFRE International does recommend that you review the content areas covered on the exam by using the CFRE Test Content Outline. It may be helpful to review the CFRE Test Content Outline for topics or subtopics with which you are less familiar. Focus your study or review on the areas with which you are least familiar. You may also want to do a surface review of all the content areas, even those you believe you know well.

To help you assess your current level of knowledge, we have prepared the Knowledge Domain Assessment Tool based on the CFRE Test Content Outline. Use it to rate yourself in each of the knowledge domains. In each area, you will decide if you have:

Level I Knowledge: I recognize the key terms and concepts of this knowledge domain but have little or no professional experience in this area.
Level II Knowledge: I understand the key terms and concepts of this knowledge domain and have had some professional experience in this area.
Level III Knowledge: I feel fairly comfortable with the key terms and concepts of this knowledge domain and have solid professional experience and/or have engaged in some formal study of best practices in this area.

	DOMAIN	LEVEL I	LEVEL II	LEVEL III
	Current & Prospective Donor Research			
1	Develop a list of prospective donors by identifying individuals, groups, and entities, such as foundations, corporations, and government agencies, with the linkage, ability, and interest to give in order to qualify prospective donors for further research and cultivation.			
2	Implement and utilize a secure data management system to ensure data privacy, store information on current and prospective donors, and enable segmented retrieval and analysis.			
3	Collect and analyze current and prospective donor information including demographics, psychographics, interests, values, motivations, culture, ability, giving and volunteer history, relationships, and linkages to select potential donors for particular projects and fundraising programs.			
4	Rate current and prospective donors on linkage, ability, and interest to prioritize and plan cultivation and solicitation.			
5	Communicate and validate relevant donor information with key organizational stakeholders to establish a plan of action for engagement, cultivation, solicitation, and stewardship.			
	Securing the Gift			
1	Develop a case for support by involving stakeholders in order to communicate the rationale for supporting the organization's mission.			
2	Identify solicitation strategies and techniques appropriate to current and prospective donor groups.			
3	Develop and implement specific solicitation plans for the involvement of individual donors, donor groups, and/or entities.			
4	Prepare donor-focused solicitation communications in order to facilitate informed gift decisions.			
5	Ask for and secure gifts from current and prospective donors in order to generate financial support for the organization's mission.			
	Relationship Building			
1	Initiate and strengthen relationships with constituents through systematic cultivation and stewardship plans designed to build trust in, and long-term commitment to, the organization.			
2	Develop and implement a comprehensive communications plan to inform constituents about the organization's mission, vision, values, financial and ethical practices, funding priorities, and gift opportunities.			
3	Promote a culture of philanthropy by broadening constituents' understanding of the value of giving.			
4	Acknowledge and recognize donor gifts and engagement in ways that are meaningful to donors and appropriate to the mission and values of the organization.			
	Volunteer Involvement			
1	Identify organizational readiness and opportunities to engage volunteers.			
2	Create structured processes for the identification, recruitment, orientation, training, evaluation, recognition, retention, and succession of volunteers.			
3	Develop specific role descriptions and terms of commitment to empower and support volunteers and enhance their effectiveness.			
4	Engage various types of volunteers (for example, board, program, campaign) in the fundraising process to increase organizational capacity.			
5	Participate in recruiting experienced and diverse leadership on boards and/or committees to ensure these groups are representative of, and responsive to, the communities served.			
	Leadership & Management			
1	Demonstrate leadership that advances fundraising practice.			
2	Advocate for and support a culture of philanthropy and the advancement of fundraising across the organization and its constituencies.			
3	Ensure that sound administrative and management policies and procedures are in place to support fundraising functions.			
4	Participate in the organization's strategic planning process to ensure the integration of fundraising and philanthropy.			
5	Design and implement short- and long-term fundraising plans and budgets to support the organization's strategic goals.			
6	Employ marketing and public relations principles and tools to support and grow fundraising programs.			
7	Conduct ongoing performance measurement and analysis of fundraising programs using accepted and appropriate standards and metrics in order to identify opportunities, resolve problems, and inform future planning.			
8	Recruit, train, and support staff by providing professional development opportunities and applying human resource principles to foster professionalism and a productive, team-oriented work environment.			
9	Utilize external services as needed to optimize the efforts of the fundraising function.			
	Ethics, Accountability, & Professionalism			
1	Ensure that all fundraising activities and policies comply with ethical principles and legal standards and reflect the values of the organization and the community.			
2	Communicate principles of ethical fundraising to stakeholders to promote ethical practices and strengthen a culture of philanthropy.			
3	Promote ethical fundraising as a crucial component of philanthropy to strengthen the nonprofit sector and support the sector's role as a pillar of civil society.			
4	Clarify, implement, monitor, and honor donors' intent and instructions regarding the use of gifts.			
5	Ensure that allocations of donations are accurately documented in the organization's records.			
6	Report to constituents the sources, uses, impact, and management of donations to demonstrate transparency and enhance public trust in the organization.			
7	Participate as an active and contributing member of the fundraising profession through activities such as mentoring, continuing education, research, and membership in professional associations.			

Developing a Study Plan

Every fundraising professional is different, with unique job experiences, professional responsibilities, and opportunities for fundraising education. There is not a single best way to prepare for the CFRE exam. The steps below are offered only as a helpful guide and not as a prescriptive list.

1. Review the Test Content Outline against what your own professional experience has been.
2. Once you have identified areas for review, do some or all of the following activities (depending on your learning style and preferences):
   1. Attend a CFRE Exam Compass course or another continuing education program on review topics.
   2. Select and read a publication from the CFRE Resource Reading List (found in Part III of this guide) that addresses the areas you have identified.
   3. Form an informal study group with other colleagues in the area planning to take the CFRE Exam. You can benefit from the diverse experience of others and provide an alternate perspective. The CFRE Central Online Community is a good place to connect with others who are preparing to take the exam. Visit **https://central.cfre.org/home**.
   4. Review materials independently, determining for yourself on which content areas you should focus.
   5. Participate in more structured review environments, perhaps with individuals who already are CFREs.

While there is not one best way to study, it is important to develop your own individual plan. Beginning several weeks prior to the exam, set aside some time each week to devote to some form of preparation.

Some candidates may choose to review the basic texts and try to absorb as much factual information as possible. If you find this type of studying effective, you might want to create index cards in the form of questions and answers or with key topics. You can test yourself or work with a friend or colleague who can quiz you until you know the answers to all the cards.

This type of study can be effective and the examination will have questions which deal with strictly factual information. However, the CFRE exam is testing the application of best practices on the job which will require you to analyze and interpret data, solve problems, and/or make judgments. With these types of questions, you will need to begin by recalling factual information, but you will then need to do something more. As a result, your study efforts should include time spent on applying factual knowledge and reviewing how it assists you in performing your duties on a daily basis.

Don't wait until the last minute to study. A hasty, tense reading of a wealth of information will not be effective. A late-hour "cram session" the night before the exam may only make you anxious and tired the next morning and hinder your ability to focus on the exam. So, for the most satisfactory and successful preparation experience, develop your plan early and follow it consistently.

Planning Worksheet

Personal Learning Preferences

My preferred methods of learning are:

I would rank my ability and comfort with test taking as (circle one):
1. Highly comfortable
2. Somewhat comfortable
3. I feel neutral
4. Somewhat uncomfortable
5. Highly uncomfortable

Why do I feel this way about test taking? What can I do to make myself more comfortable/prepared as a test taker?

Resources For Test Preparation

I plan to use the following resources to prepare myself for the CFRE exam:

I plan to seek help/input from the following people as I prepare:

Section Two

Learning to Think Like a CFRE

A CFRE is a confident, ethical fundraising professional who is knowledgeable about and abides by best practices in ethical fundraising. While the CFRE Test Content Outline shows the knowledge domains you need to know as a fundraising professional, it also shows—but does not do so explicitly— the importance of understanding the connections among the knowledge domains and how all fundraising best practice is based on ethical principles.

At a macro level, this section focuses on helping build your understanding of the fundamental principles of ethical fundraising—principles to which you will refer time and again as you think through the questions on the CFRE exam. At a micro level, this section will help you apply these principles as you grow your test-taking confidence. Keep both aspects in mind as you study for and take the CFRE exam.

Best Practices in Ethical Fundraising: An Overview

Fundraising is a values exchange that exists within the complex set of stakeholders and relationships that comprise the philanthropic sector. Within this context, there are three essential "value commitments" that the fundraising professional must consider, work with, and balance:

1. Organizational mission.
2. Relationships with stakeholders.
3. The fundraising professional's own sense of professional and personal integrity.[4]

At all times, "the fund raiser [sic], acting with integrity, has the task of creating and maintaining a supporting network of relationships in order to further the mission of the organization."[5]

While ethics can sometimes be a gray area where reasonable people can reasonably disagree about the exact course of action to be taken, one thing is clear: There can be no best practice unless fundraising professionals are knowledgeable about and abide by generally agreed upon ethical principles for fundraising.

Because the CFRE certification program is dedicated to best practices in ethical fundraising, and the CFRE Test Content Outline shows the blueprint of best practices in ethical fundraising, individuals aspiring to CFRE certification need to know core precepts of fundraising ethics. The International Statement of Ethical Principles in Fundraising and the Donor Bill of Rights are two important documents outlining best practices in ethical fundraising. As you study them, think about what they share in common and how they provide insight into how the "value commitments" of fundraising are enacted in the daily work of the fundraising professional. Also think about what you need to know regarding laws regulating fundraising and the conduct expected of a CFRE.

International Statement of Ethical Principles in Fundraising

While most associations serving fundraising professionals have developed codes of ethics specific to their members, the International Statement of Ethical Principles in Fundraising articulates the core elements of fundraising best practices and ethics worldwide.

The International Statement of Ethical Principles in Fundraising was first ratified at the International Fundraising Summit in 2006 by fundraising associations representing 24 nations. The International Statement documents the common principles of ethical fundraising around the globe. The current version of this statement was adopted at the International Fundraising Summit held in July 2018. As part of the CFRE application process, CFRE candidates attest that they are knowledgeable about and abide by the International Statement of Ethical Principles in Fundraising.

In brief, the International Statement states fundraising professionals will define their ethical approach by acting with honesty, respect, integrity, transparency, and responsibility toward their stakeholders. The International Statement identifies these areas of concern that are at the heart of standards of practice for fundraising excellence:

1. Responsibility to fully comply with relevant legislations and regulatory standards.
2. Responsibility to supporters.
3. Responsibility to their [fundraising professionals'] cause and beneficiaries.
4. Management reporting, finance, and fundraising costs.
5. Pay and compensation.

International Statement of Ethical Principles in Fundraising (Revised July 2018)

All over the globe, fundraisers work to make the world a better place. Our causes are diverse and distinct, but our passion and commitment are universal. The way that we go about raising money is different according to the culture, society, and laws of where we fundraise, but we share a commitment that wherever we fundraise, we do so to a high standard and follow an ethical approach.

This Statement of Ethical Principles in Fundraising sets out the values, beliefs, and principles that govern professional fundraisers across the world. It sets out what unites us in the way that we fundraise and joins us together as a global fundraising community dedicated to achieving fundraising excellence for our causes, donors, and supporters.

The Statement does not replicate, replace, or supersede any laws or codes of conduct that are in place in any individual country, as it is expected that fundraisers will fully observe the law wherever they work. Instead, the Statement outlines the ethical approach and articulates the values that drive fundraising professionals and provides a framework of how we will work globally. Organizations that voluntarily endorse and support this Statement do so as a demonstration of their commitment to fundraising excellence and as a declaration of their shared interest in a global understanding of these principles.

Where fundraisers are working in areas with a developed code of conduct, this Statement should complement the standards that are set, and for others can form a basis for the development of fundraising practice or regulation. By following these principles, we believe that we will deliver the best experience for our donors and supporters, grow public trust and confidence in fundraising, and be best placed to achieve our mission.

Our Shared Principles For Fundraising

As fundraisers, these principles set out how we work and define our ethical approach:

Honesty: Fundraisers will always be honest and truthful, upholding public trust and never misleading supporters or the public.

Respect: Fundraisers will always be respectful of our beneficiaries and donors, following their choices and wishes, wherever possible.

Integrity: Fundraisers will always act with integrity, following legislative and regulatory requirements, and will always work for the best interests of our causes and supporters.

Transparency: Fundraisers will always be transparent, clear, and accurate about the work of our causes, how donations will be managed and spent, and report on costs and impact accurately.

Responsibility: Fundraisers will always act responsibly, understanding that we share a common objective to promote fundraising excellence for the benefit of the common good.

We value and encourage diversity in our practice and our fundraisers, and continually seek to develop our professional standards.

Standards Of Fundraising Practice

Our standards are presented as being the benchmark for fundraising excellence and set out our shared framework for working to the highest level and in the best interests of our causes, while respecting our donors and being accountable in our work.

1. Responsibility to fully comply with relevant legislation and regulatory standards
    - Fundraisers will work according to the national and international legal obligations that apply to their organization's location, legal form, and activities.
    - Fundraisers will follow any agreed upon regulatory systems for fundraising and specific codes of practice for fundraising that are set in their location.

Fundraisers will not take action that could constitute professional misconduct or create a conflict of interest.

2. Responsibility to supporters
    - Fundraisers will always respect the free choice of all individuals to give donations or not.
    - Fundraisers will respect the rights of donors and follow their preferences on communications and privacy.
    - Fundraisers will be open and transparent with donors on the use of their funds, providing clear information on how donations are spent and the impact of their work.
    - Fundraisers will be truthful and honest in all of their fundraising communications, in any medium and by any means, using accurate information about their cause in their materials, communications, and activities.
    - Where a donor has expressed a view on the specific service or project that they would like their money to be applied, the donor's wishes will be followed wherever possible.
    - In the event that the money cannot be used in line with the donor's wishes, the fundraiser will seek further agreement from the individual or organization on the use of their donation.

3. Responsibility to their cause and beneficiaries
   - Fundraisers will work together with their trustees or relevant governance structure to best achieve the overall goals and objectives of their cause, making decisions and working in accordance with the values of the organization.
   - Fundraisers will always be respectful of their beneficiaries and uphold their dignity and self-respect in the fundraising communications or materials that they use.
   - Fundraisers will not accept donations where the acceptance of those gifts would not be in the best interests of the organization or create a conflict of interest that would be detrimental to the organization's reputation, mission, and relationship with existing supporters and beneficiaries.

4. Management reporting, finance, and fundraising costs
   - Fundraisers will be transparent and accurate in presenting fundraising costs, fees, and expenses, without expressing or suggesting in communications and materials that fundraising lacks administration and fundraising costs.
   - Fundraisers will ensure that all fundraising transactions, accounting, and reporting for which they are responsible are transparent and accurate.
   - Fundraisers will work with their organization to provide accurate reports on their organization's income and expenditure according to their national regulatory framework, and publish clear information on their activities for stakeholders, beneficiaries, donors, and the public.

5. Pay and compensation
   - Fundraisers will expect fair remuneration for their work and will not use their position to make any unauthorized or disproportionate personal gain.
   - Fundraisers will not seek any personal benefits or gratuities in the course of their work. Any benefits or gratuities that are offered to a fundraiser will be declared to their organization and/or any relevant authority and only accepted if in line with the set policy and with any necessary approval.
   - When fundraisers work with suppliers, partners, or third-party agencies, they will take all reasonable steps to ensure that those external parties work to the same standards that they are held to, and that they do not receive unreasonable and disproportionate payment for their work.
   - All payment and remuneration for fundraisers will be arranged before work is carried out, with any performance-related payments agreed in advance and set to ensure that payments will not be disproportionate or unreasonable.

Agreed by representatives of National Fundraising Associations and adopted at the International Fundraising Summit in London on 7 July 2018

Understanding the Donor Bill of Rights

The Donor Bill of Rights outlines the transparency due in interactions with donors in order to strengthen trust in fundraising and philanthropy. The Donor Bill of Rights was created in 1993 by the Association of Fundraising Professionals (AFP), the Association for Healthcare Philanthropy (AHP), the Council for Advancement and Support of Education (CASE), and the Giving Institute: Leading Consultants to Non-Profits. It has been endorsed by numerous organizations. Even if your fundraising association does not formally endorse the Donor Bill of Rights, it is important to know the document's key principles because they constitute a valuable overview of best practices in ethical fundraising in matters of transparency, accountability, and reporting to donors regarding the organization's work and the use of gifts.

The Donor Bill of Rights

Philanthropy is based on voluntary action for the common good. It is a tradition of giving and sharing that is primary to the quality of life. To assure that philanthropy merits the respect and trust of the general public, and that donors and prospective donors can have full confidence in the not-for-profit organizations and causes they are asked to support, we declare that all donors have these rights:

I. To be informed of the organization's mission, of the way the organization intends to use donated resources, and of its capacity to use donations effectively for their intended purposes.

II. To be informed of the identity of those serving on the organization's governing board, and to expect the board to exercise prudent judgment in its stewardship responsibilities.

III. To have access to the organization's most recent financial statements.

IV. To be assured their gifts will be used for the purposes for which they were given.

V. To receive appropriate acknowledgement and recognition.

VI. To be assured that information about their donation is handled with respect and with confidentiality to the extent provided by law.

VII. To expect that all relationships with individuals representing organizations of interest to the donor will be professional in nature.

VIII. To be informed whether those seeking donations are volunteers, employees of the organization, or hired solicitors.

IX. To have the opportunity for their names to be deleted from mailing lists that an organization may intend to share.

X. To feel free to ask questions when making a donation and to receive prompt, truthful, and forthright answers.

*Reprinted with permission from the Association of Fundraising Professionals.

Knowledge of and Adherence to Laws Regulating Fundraising

As part of the application process, all CFRE candidates must attest that they are knowledgeable about and abide by the laws regulating fundraising in their geographical area(s) of practice. Generally, these laws deal with issues regarding:

- Charity and charitable solicitation registration.
- Means of conducting charitable solicitations.
- Truthfulness and transparency in charitable solicitations.
- Reporting and accounting standards.
- Taxation.

Fundraising professionals who are not confident that they are knowledgeable about the laws regulating fundraising in their geographical area(s) of practice should consult the fundraising association(s) of which they are members for further information and/or government agencies charged with the above issues.

The knowledge of and adherence to laws regulating fundraising is a vital part of best practice. However, the CFRE exam does not include country-specific questions because the CFRE certification program offers a single global exam that is available in countries around the world, each of which has different laws and agencies regulating fundraising practice.

CFRE Accountability Standards

CFRE International also has its own set of standards regarding the integrity of the CFRE certification program. CFRE Accountability Standards require all CFRE candidates and certification holders to be accurate, truthful, and complete in their CFRE applications; be accurate in making statements about their certification status; not misuse CFRE designation or trademarks and report misuse by others; maintain the confidentiality of CFRE exam content; and comply with all ethical and professional standards adopted by the professional associations to which they belong.

See Appendix III for *CFRE Accountability Standards*.

In Summary

Ethics lies at the heart of all fundraising best practices. As you move forward in studying the six domains of fundraising knowledge contained in the CFRE Test Content Outline, be sure to consider and articulate the ethical principles upon which accepted best practice is founded. This will support your efforts to prepare successfully for the CFRE exam.

Section Three

Understanding the Knowledge Domains

Domain 1:
Current & Prospective Donor Research
(15% of total scored items—26 items)

Introduction

Information is the most valuable commodity we have in fundraising. Our success is largely dependent on how we gather, organize, interpret, and deploy information. As such, current and prospective donor research is a critical component of the body of knowledge essential to fundraising.

Donor research is not just about numbers. It is the paint with which we create profiles of individual donors, donor segments, and future donors. While donor research provides us with a reasonable framework for approaching our donors and their philanthropic goals and values, it also tells us where our organization aligns with those goals and values.

Recommended Reading

The publications on the Reading Resource List are all widely available and provide information on current, commonly accepted fundraising practices. These references have been identified as being the most comprehensive and most closely related to information covered on the examination.

It is not intended that each candidate read every publication on the Resource Reading List. Rather, this list is provided as a guide for candidates who are seeking sources of information on particular subject areas, or general overview texts. Reading any or all of the publications on this list does not guarantee you will do well on the examination.

- *Keep Your Donors (2008)* by Tom Ahern and Simone Joyaux

- *Beyond Fund Raising, 2nd Edition (2005)* by Kay Sprinkel Grace

- *Visual Planned Giving: An Introduction To The Law & Taxation Of Charitable Gift Planning (2014)* by Dr. Russell James III

- *Capital Campaigns: Strategies That Work 4th Edition (2016)* by Andrea Kihlstedt

- *Fundraising Basics: A Complete Guide: A Complete Guide 3rd Edition (2009)* by Barbara L. Ciconte and Jeanne Jacob

- *Fundraising Principles and Practice, 3rd Edition (2024)* by Adrian Sargeant, Jen Shang

- *Achieving Excellence in Fundraising 5th Edition (2022)* by Genevieve G. Shaker, Eugene R. Tempel, et al.

- *Fundraising for Social Change, 8th Edition (2022)* by Kim Klein, Stan Yogi

Key Terms & Concepts

Ability A donor's ability to give is an assessment of their financial capacity, stage of life, and the liquidity of their assets. Ability is often mistakenly tied to perceived income, which may not always be an accurate indicator of ability to give.

Cultivation Cultivation is a series of activities to maintain and deepen relationships and engagement with donors, prospective donors, and volunteers.

Data Mining Data mining is the process of collecting, researching, analyzing, and segmenting information about donors, prospective donors, and volunteers.

Data Privacy Data privacy is the responsibility of the nonprofit organization to maintain secure digital records and to fully disclose any sharing of information with third-party organizations upon the acceptance of an individual's information.[6]

Demographics Demographics refer to the statistical data of a population, including age, income, education, political affiliation, marital and family status, etc.[7]

Donor Profile A donor profile is a concise record of an individual's linkage, ability, and interest in an organization. It contains verified contact info, giving history, and wealth indicators.[8]

Donor Qualifying Qualifying is the ongoing process of assessing linkage, ability, and interest of your donors in order to match them with the right program, appeal, and amount.

Donor Rating Rating is the process by which current donors are evaluated by staff and volunteers (board members) for their capacity to make a gift of significance (major gift, planned gift, lead gift, etc.)

Engagement Two definitions for "engage" in the dictionary are "to attract and hold fast," and "to occupy the attention or efforts of a person or persons." For the nonprofit, engagement means an ongoing effort to learn about your donors, communicate with them, and offer shared experiences (volunteering, events, etc.).[9]

Frequency Frequency refers to how often a donor gives, and to which repeated appeals.

Giving History A donor's giving history is the sum total of a donor's giving records. This includes frequency, renewal rate, appeal responses, average gift, highest gift, most recent gift, etc.

Interest A donor or prospective donor's level of interest correlates to their likelihood of making a gift. Interest, from the nonprofit viewpoint, is the combination of concern, excitement, motivation, and engagement an individual has for your organization's mission.

Lifetime Donor Value *The lifetime projected value* of a donor is an estimate of total current and future contributions to your organization. It is typically determined by multiplying lifespan times average donation amount times frequency of donation.[10] Value = Lifespan x Amount x Frequency.

The *lifetime actual value* of a donor is simply the sum of all recorded gifts for that donor.

Linkage Linkage refers to the connections a donor or prospective donor has to your organization and/or its mission. These could be in the form of experience (former alum, program participant), connections with people (friend, relative, colleagues), shared values (advocacy, stage of life), and personal history.

Market Research Market research refers to the process of gathering, organizing, and interpreting data regarding donor and prospective donor preferences, attitudes, interests, and giving ability.

Prospect A prospect or prospective donor is one who has been evaluated based on donor research and found to have a connection to the organization, the ability to give an appropriate level, and an interest in the organization's mission.

Key Terms & Concepts continued

Renewal rates An organization's renewal rate is the percentage of donors who make a subsequent gift to the organization. Often tracked to a specific appeal (such as those who renew to an annual appeal) or tracked by giving in general (those who give any gift to any appeal after their initial gift). Renewal rates are often a reflection of how well the organization thanks its donors and keeps them informed of how gifts are used. Also known as attrition rates.

Segmentation Segmentation is the process of grouping donors and prospective donors into like categories in order to more efficiently allocate resources and target appeals. Donors can be segmented by giving levels, giving history, program interest, likely response format (email vs mail appeal for example), and other groups.

Solicitation History The solicitation history of a donor is a record of all donation requests made by the organization whether they are successful or not. It includes both mass appeals (email, direct mail, etc.) and in-person asks of any size. An accurate solicitation history allows the organization to make informed decisions about resource allocation and subsequent requests.

Domain Content Review

To master the key concept areas of Current and Prospective Donor Research on the CFRE exam, a fundraising professional must be able to:

1.1 Develop a list of prospective donors by identifying individuals, groups, and entities (such as foundations, corporations, and government agencies) with organizational linkage, ability to give, and interest in the cause for further research and cultivation.
1.2 Implement, maintain, and utilize a secure data management system to ensure data privacy, store information on current and prospective donors, and enable segmented retrieval and analysis.
1.3 Collect and analyze current and prospective donor information (such as demographics, psychographics, interests, values, motivations, culture, ability, giving and volunteer history, relationships, and linkages) to select potential donors for particular projects and fundraising programs.
1.4 Qualify and rate current and prospective donors on linkage, ability, and interest to prioritize and plan cultivation and solicitation.
1.5 Communicate and validate relevant donor information with key organizational stakeholders to establish a plan of action for engagement, cultivation, solicitation, and stewardship.

Self-Assessment

Using the key term and concepts, the recommended reading materials at the beginning of this chapter, the *International Statement of Ethical Principles in Fundraising*, and the *Donor Bill of Rights*, take a moment to assess your understanding of these key knowledge areas:

▸ Indicators that identify trends and define characteristics that assist in determining giving potential:

▸ Donor acquisition and retention principles:

▸ Sources of financial support such as individuals, corporations, grant-making bodies, foundations, governmental agencies, and gaming:

▸ Types of information needed to identify prospective donors and determine specific fundraising strategies:

▸ Donor profile components:

▸ Indicators of the donor's ability to give, organizational linkage, and interest in the cause:

▸ Donor giving patterns such as recency, frequency, renewal rates, and monetary value:

▸ Data analysis techniques such as statistical analysis, data mining, and segmentation:

▸ Data gathering techniques such as surveys, focus groups, interviews, and social networking:

▸ Elements of a comprehensive data management system including data capture, storage, retrieval, maintenance, and security:

▸ Prospective donor screening, qualifying, and rating methods:

- Motivations, practices, and policies of various funding sources:

- Prospective donor information sources such as people, written or published sources, and electronic or online sources, and their uses and limitations:

- Elements or components of a fundraising program, including annual giving, capital/major giving, and planned giving/legacies:

- Relationships between and among annual giving, capital/major giving, and planned giving/legacies programs:

- Market research components and uses:

- Privacy legislation and regulation:

▶ Ethical use of data:

▶ Elements of engagement, cultivation, solicitation, and stewardship plans:

Study Questions

This section is meant to help you become familiar with the type of questions that you may encounter on the CFRE exam. Additional questions are found at the end of each knowledge domain chapter and in the CFRE Practice Exam.

Answers to the questions below can be found in Appendix II.

Questions

1. In setting up a fundraising program focused on foundations for a new organization, the first step is to:
   A. Make appointments for key volunteers to meet with foundation board members.
   B. Make an appointment for the chief executive officer to meet with foundation leadership.
   C. Call on all foundations that you have previously worked with to let them know of the new cause.
   D. Research foundations that give to similar organizations and follow up.

2. The primary purpose of rating an organization's donors is to determine their:
   A. Interest in the organization's cause.
   B. Involvement in the organization.
   C. Willingness to give to the organization.
   D. Potential to give to the organization.

3. The process of establishing the financial range of gifts that a donor will reasonably consider is referred to as:
   A. Rating.
   B. Determination.
   C. Research.
   D. Cultivating.

4. Foundation prospects for an organization are best identified by the geographic scope of the foundation, its granting criteria, and the foundation's:
   A. Board.
   B. Previous giving history.
   C. Most recent award.
   D. Capacity for grants.

5. Prospective donors for an organization are best identified by:
   A. Apparent philanthropic interest.
   B. The organization's past and current board members.
   C. Interest in the organization's services.
   D. Links with the organization, giving ability, and interest.

Current & Prospective Donor Research Additional Review

Now that you have completed this chapter, outline any areas that will require more preparation and study:

Additional Best Practices

Prospect research is:

- **Ongoing:** Donor information is constantly changing, and every effort should be made to maintain accurate up-to-date records.
- **Selective:** Donors and their interests should be segmented for efficiency and relevance.
- **Confidential:** Every effort should be made to protect donor data and confidentiality.
- **Accurate:** Information should be attributable and verified.
- **Personal:** The percentage of information that is supplied by and verified by the donor themselves should increase over time.
- **Relevant:** Research should coincide with funding needs.

Prospect Data List. The following items are typically found in a donor profile.[11]

- Name, nickname
- Salutation
- Home address
- Business name, job title, address
- Home phone
- Work phone
- Date & place of birth
- Education
- Job history
- Marital status
- Spouse name/business
- Number, name, ages of children
- Connections to the organization
- Connections to other organizations
- Board service & volunteer history
- Honors/achievements/awards
- Political affiliations
- Religious affiliations
- Personal interests
- Net worth
- Net salary
- Stock holdings
- Directorships
- Gift records
- Names of business associates (attorney/financial planner/admin assistant)
- Relevant friends

Contact reports typically include[12]

- Date
- Place & reason for last contact
- Result of last contact
- Next steps and assigning tasks

Questions To Ask When Profiling A Donor
- Do we have the most recent & up to date information?
- Are there wealth indicators or financial assessments available on the donor?
- How does the donor/prospect use their wealth?
- Based on the current known information, what is the individual's giving capacity?
- What is the prospect's linkage & interest to your organization?
- Who is the best person or persons to establish and cultivate a relationship?[13]

Donor Rating Best Practices
- Donor rating is part of the ongoing evaluation of your donor base.
- Donor rating is typically done by staff and separately by volunteers in order to validate the findings.
- The donor rating process is not focused on what a donor may give or will give, rather on what a donor can give.
- During the volunteer rating process, staff may be present to record the findings, but should not be involved in the discussion.
- These can be conducted in a variety of ways, but the most common are:
    - Group discussions, group/individual ratings, and individual evaluations.
    - Evaluations should be done by knowledgeable individuals and not rely on second-hand information.

Standard Donor Database Reports[14]
- **Comparison Report:** Compare giving totals and donor population for the current and previous years.
- **Pledge Report:** Analysis of pledge amounts, completion, and past due status.
- **Productivity Report:** An analysis of month-to-month giving results, year-to-year giving results, and previous three fiscal year giving comparison.
- **Giving Analysis:** Listing of the number of donors and total giving at all giving levels that the organization tracks during the past year.
- **Multi-Year Giving Trends:** Long-term analysis of donor population and giving amounts.

Prospect Research Types

Proactive Research

Geodemographic Segmentation: Comparing the donors in your database against the characteristics of their region (neighbors, ZIP/postal code, town, county, etc.) and consumer behavior models to assess their lifestyles, giving trends, and interests.[15]

Asset Screening: Comparing your donor database to publicly reported stock holdings, property ownership, and company ownership (private & public).

Financial Rating: A staff/organization driven rating of a donor's potential to give and the probable gift size.

Peer Screening: A donor rating process facilitated by staff but conducted by volunteers (board members) to rate their peer's potential and probability to give. During the process volunteers also discuss what relevant information they have on the donors in question.[16]

Digital Sources: Online sources such as LinkedIn and other social media sites can be used to gather information about donors, their philanthropic interests, and their linkages to members of your board, leadership, and staff.

Reactive Research

Linkage: The extent to which the prospect is connected to your organization.

Ability: The prospect's capacity to give now and in the future.

Interest: The level to which your organization's mission aligns with the philanthropic goals of the prospect.

Corporate Giving Research

The first step in securing a gift from a company is to understand the vehicle by which they make donations.

Types of Corporate (or small company) Giving

- Foundations
- Matching Gifts
- Research & Development
- Marketing & Advertising
- Discretionary Budget

Questions to Ask When Researching a Company

- What is the financial health of the company?
- What are their products and services and how do they align with your organization?
- What existing relationships or linkages can be used to increase the likelihood of a gift?
- Has the company supported you in the past?
- What other organizations does the company support?
- What compelling aspect of your organization or mission would make this company likely to support you now or in the future?

Domain 2
Securing the Gift
(22% of total scored items—39 items)

Introduction

Securing any gift is an ongoing process and includes the creation of a development plan, case for support, and the communications plan. With these three fundamental documents serving as a solid foundation and road map for a solicitation, a variety of techniques can be deployed to secure the gift. The piece that provides the infrastructure to fundraising is the case for support. The Case answers these questions:
- Who is the organization?
- What community need are they attempting to address?
- Why is the organization worthy of support?
- Why is this organization the best to solve this societal need?

Recommended Reading

The publications on the Reading Resource List are all widely available and provide information on current, commonly accepted fundraising practices. These references have been identified as being the most comprehensive and most closely related to information covered on the examination.

It is not intended that each candidate read every publication on the Resource Reading List. Rather, this list is provided as a guide for candidates who are seeking sources of information on particular subject areas, or general overview texts. Reading any or all of the publications on this list does not guarantee you will do well on the examination.

- *The Fundraising Reader (2023)* by Beth Breeze, Pamela Wiepking, Donna Day Lafferty

- *Keep Your Donors (2008)* by Tom Ahern and Simone Joyaux

- *Beyond Fund Raising, 2nd Edition (2005)* by Kay Sprinkel Grace

- *Visual Planned Giving: An Introduction To The Law & Taxation Of Charitable Gift Planning (2014)* by Dr. Russell James III

- *Capital Campaigns: Strategies That Work 4th Edition (2016)* by Andrea Kihlstedt

- *Fundraising Basics: A Complete Guide: A Complete Guide 3rd Edition (2009)* by Barbara L. Ciconte and Jeanne Jacob

- *Fundraising Principles and Practice, 3rd Edition (2024)* by Adrian Sargeant, Jen Shang

- *Achieving Excellence in Fundraising 5th Edition (2022)* by Genevieve G. Shaker, Eugene R. Tempel, et al.

- *Fundraising for Social Change, 8th Edition (2022)* by Kim Klein, Stan Yogi

Key Terms & Concepts

Average Gift Average gift is calculated by dividing the total money raised by the number of gifts given. Organizations often track this statistic for both the entire donor base as well as for individual donors.

Capital Campaign A structured fundraising effort (outside the annual campaign) to secure significant gifts and pledges during a defined timeframe for unique purposes such as buildings, endowments, or equipment.[17]

Capital Gift A charitable contribution designated or intended for the purchase and/or construction of a new building or property, or the improvement and/or renovation of an existing building, property, or physical space.

Case for Support The collection of information that illustrates why an organization is worthy of support.

Cause Marketing When a company donates to an organization in an amount that correlates to the number of individual purchases of the company's product or services during a defined period of time.[18]

Corporate Sponsorship A gift of cash or in-kind goods or services by a corporate entity in return for access and recognition at an event or cause.[19]

Cost of Fundraising The sum of expenses related to fundraising efforts. These include salaries, payroll taxes and benefits, supplies, marketing and advertising, occupancy costs, and other costs related to development.

Cost Per Dollar Raised Cost per dollar raised calculates the total cost to yield a single dollar of revenue. Also called Cost to Raise a Dollar (CTRD). It is the inverse of Return on Investment (ROI).

Direct Marketing Physical marketing materials such as letters, flyers, catalogs, etc.

Elements of an Effective Case A mission statement, goals, objectives, description of programs and services, finances, governance structure, staffing and organization chart, facilities and service delivery description, planning and evaluation, and organizational history.[20]

Endowment Gift Gift of cash, investment funds, or property to an organization for the purpose of investing the principal while using the dividends or other resulting investment income for charitable purposes.[21]

Feasibility Study The formal process of determining both organizational readiness and potential constituency support for a capital campaign or project. These are typically performed by a third-party consultant or company that specializes in this area. During the study, the consultant attempts to determine:
- Does a compelling case for support exist?
- Is there management and staff infrastructure to support the campaign?
- Is there sufficient board buy-in?
- Is there sufficient donor interest and giving capacity to support the campaign and its fundraising priorities and goals?

Gift Agreement A formal arrangement between a donor and the recipient which spells out the nature of the gift, how it is to be used, and how the gift will be acknowledged.

Gifts In-Kind Gifts of tangible goods or services as opposed to gifts of funds to purchase goods or services.

Gift of Property A gift of property includes any gift of real estate. Examples include homes, farmland, commercial property, and undeveloped land.

Grant Proposal Writing Process of responding to a request for proposal (RFP) from a foundation, corporation, or government agency. Grant proposals follow a specified format established by the funding organization and typically include organizational information, a case statement, program information, budget, projected outcomes, and an evaluation process. May also refer to proposals submitted in the absence of an RFP but when the funding agency's stated goals align with the applicant organization's and the agency accepts unsolicited proposals.

Lead Gift A significant donation (10% of the goal of a capital campaign or annual fund) that establishes the campaign and sets a benchmark for others capable of giving at a similar level.[22]

Key Terms & Concepts continued

Memorial and Tribute Gifts Philanthropic gifts made to an organization in honor of another person (typically deceased for memorial gifts; typically living for tribute gifts).

Nucleus Gift A major gift given in the initial stages of a campaign, typically at the start of a campaign.[23]

Payroll Giving A system where pre-tax deductions are made from an employee's paycheck and given directly to a nonprofit organization.

Peer-to-Peer Fundraising When an individual personally fundraises directly from their friends, network, or peer group for a specific organization or cause. The organization may control the payment platform and/or support for the messaging; however, the individual controls when, where, and to whom the messages are delivered.

Pledge and Installments A pledge to give a specific amount of money monthly, quarterly, or annually for a set number of months and/or years. While typically used in capital campaigns, it is also used in major gift fundraising and in annual funds.

Response Rate Refers to the percentage of recipients who received a piece of physical mail, an email, or a telephone call who respond with a gift or by taking another action requested by the organization, such as signing up for an event or asking for more information about legacy giving.

ROI Return on Investment or the amount of revenue generated for a given strategy divided by the expenses required to generate that revenue. This is the inverse of Cost Per Dollar Raised (also called Cost to Raise a Dollar or CTRD).

Securities Includes stocks, commodities, mutual funds, and bonds.

Solicitation Plan A specific and thoughtful plan for meeting with and soliciting a gift from an individual donor. The plan can include who will accompany the gift officer (solicitation team), who will speak when, what support or collateral materials will be included, what objections may be expected and how to address them, and what follow-up activities will take place. Solicitation materials should be specific and tailored to the potential donor.

Special Events In a fundraising context, a special event is any function designed to attract, involve, and inform people about a cause or organization.[24]

Trusts A legal vehicle in which one party (trustor) gives a second party (trustee) permission to manage assets for the benefit of an organization. These come in a variety of forms including living (while the trustor is still alive), testamentary (enacted upon death), revocable (can be modified), and irrevocable (cannot be modified or terminated).[25]

Ultimate Gift The largest single gift given by a donor.[26]

Domain Content Review

As a guide for studying for the exam, CFRE International has adopted a content outline for each of the six knowledge domains. To master the key concept areas of Securing the Gift on the CFRE exam, a fundraising professional must understand how to:

2.1 Develop a case for support by involving stakeholders to communicate the rationale for supporting the organization's mission.
2.2 Identify solicitation strategies, techniques, and tools appropriate to current and prospective donors.
2.3 Develop and implement specific solicitation plans for the involvement of individual donors, donor groups, and/or entities.
2.4 Prepare donor-focused solicitation communications to provide information that donors need to make gift decisions.
2.5 Ask for and secure gifts from current and prospective donors to generate financial support for the organization's mission.

Self-Assessment

Using the key term and concepts, the recommended reading materials at the beginning of this chapter, the *International Statement of Ethical Principles in Fundraising*, and the *Donor Bill of Rights*, take a moment to assess your understanding of these key knowledge areas:

▶ Psychology of giving:

▶ Sociological, cultural, and environmental influences on giving, including implications for diversity, equity, inclusion, and access:

▶ Elements of an effective case:

- Case statement construction:

- Elements of an effective solicitation plan:

- Types of gifts such as cash, securities, trusts, property, and gifts in kind:

- Solicitation strategies and their effectiveness with different donor groups:

- Components and uses of feasibility/planning studies:

- Negotiation techniques:

▶ External and internal factors that may affect the viability and/or reputation of the organization and its programs and services:

▶ Donor motivations, barriers to giving, and giving behavior:

▶ Peer relationship principles and their application to fundraising:

▶ Fundraising program evaluation standards, procedures, and methods including benchmark calculations such as cost of fundraising, Return on Investment (ROI), fundraising metrics, average gift, and response rates:

▶ Gift agreements, payment structures, and policies governing contributions such as outright gifts, pledges, and installments:

▶ Communication methods, channels, and messages to engage donors or donor groups:

▶ The use of prospect research to inform cultivation and solicitation strategies:

▶ Fundraising techniques and programs such as:
- a. Direct marketing (for example, mail, telephone, electronic, direct response television [drtv], face-to-face)
- b. Special events (for example, dinners, walk-a-thons, tournaments, auctions)
- c. Grant proposal writing (for example, foundations, corporations, government)
- d. Corporate sponsorships, partnerships, and cause-related marketing
- e. Gift planning such as bequests, legacies, and trusts
- f. Major gifts
- g. Memorial and tribute gifts
- h. Capital and endowment campaigns
- i. Membership and alumni programs
- j. Gaming and lottery programs
- k. Workforce and payroll giving, federated campaigns
- l. Community fundraising
- m. Peer-to-peer fundraising
- n. Third-party fundraising
- o. Social media campaigns
- p. Crowdfunding • Involvement of donor advisors, consultants, and legal and financial experts

Study Questions

This section is meant to help you become familiar with the type of questions that you may encounter on the CFRE exam. Additional questions are found at the end of each knowledge domain chapter and in the CFRE Practice Exam.

Answers to the questions below can be found in Appendix II.

Questions

1. In preparation of the case statement, which of the following important pieces of information should be included first?
    A. Specific objectives and goals of the organization.
    B. Mission statement of the organization.
    C. Environmental issues affecting the organization.
    D. Specific problems and needs addressed by the organization.

2. What considerations must be made when accepting a non-cash gift (securities, property, etc.)?
    A. The likelihood of the property being sold for cash.
    B. The value of the gift and tax implications of accepting it.
    C. The gift's appropriateness relative to the organization's gift acceptance policy.
    D. The timing of the gift relative to the annual campaign.

3. Who are the key stakeholders that should be involved in developing a case for support?
    A. CEO, the board chair, and the development director.
    B. Leadership, volunteers, program staff, and development staff.
    C. CEO, the board, and an outside consultant.
    D. Program staff, the board, and an outside consultant.

4. Which of the following has the best chance of success in a direct-mail program?
    A. Targeted mailing to a group of people who have a relationship to the organization.
    B. Targeted mailing to potential contributors who live in the service area and meet a certain income level.
    C. General mailing to prospects throughout the service area, both those who have and those who have not used the organization.
    D. Fundraising appeal to new residents in the service area.

5. How often should you send direct mail to your donors?
    A. Twice per month.
    B. Once per month.
    C. As many times as they respond.
    D. As often as they indicate they would like to receive mail.

Securing the Gift Additional Review

Now that you have completed this chapter, outline any areas that will require more preparation and study:

Additional Best Practices

Case Statements

The following elements should be included in a good case statement:
- A description of the organization's mission and the key community need(s) that it addresses.
- List of the organization's objectives.
- The proposed strategies for reaching those objectives and a timeline.
- Organizational assets (programs, facilities), staff, and budget needs.
- The target audience that will benefit.
- An explanation of the impact of supporting the mission and the implications if the community need is not met.
- A review of the strengths and subject matter expertise of the organization.

Additional items may include:
- Service area analysis including demographics, key industries, resources and service gaps, and organizational comparisons both locally and nationally.
- Strategic plan (if one has been done).
- An organizational chart and staff bios.
- Recent and historical giving history.
- Current and long-range needs.
- Other relevant organizational history.

Major Gift Fundraising Guidelines
- On average, the Major Gift Officer (MGO) should manage a portfolio of no more than 150 prospects.
- Time should be divided between cultivation, solicitation, and stewardship.
- On average, MGOs are expected to make 30 major gift solicitations per year resulting in 15 to 20 gifts.
- On average, MGOs are expected to qualify 15 to 25 new prospects each year to replace those who have been removed from the prospect list.

Key Elements of a Successful Capital Campaign[27]
- Feasibility study.
- Commitment of time & support from all key stakeholders.
- A strategic plan.
- A clearly articulated case for support.
- A donor base that is willing and able to commit to substantial lead gifts before the public phase of the campaign.
- Competent staff and/or the help of outside counsel.
- An adequate budget for campaign expenses.

Donor Motivations
- Awareness of the need and a desire to help the recipients.
- Trust in the organization and its ability to use the gift effectively and responsibly.
- A sense of duty.
- Tax benefits.
- Routine giving is most impacted by a personal connection to the cause or organization (friend or family member, personally impacted).
- The top motivator for unexpected giving is a personal connection or crisis.[28]
- The number two motivator for online giving: social media influencers, celebrities, and politicians.[29]

Barriers to Giving
- A poorly defined and/or articulated case for support.
- Trust in the organization.
- Poor stewardship.
- Lack of communication with donors.
- Lack of demonstrated impact.

Types of Gifts
- Cash from the donor's own accounts or accounts in which the donor has an advisory role (Donor-Advised Funds, Qualified Charitable Distributions, family foundation grants, etc.)
- In-Kind.
- Securities (stocks & bonds).
- Trusts.
- Real Estate: Commercial or residential.
- Assets (financial): retirement accounts, life insurance policies, etc.
- Assets (tangible): jewelry, art, cars, etc.

Elements of a Feasibility Study
- The feasibility study is a tool and a process to help an organization determine its institutional readiness to engage in a capital campaign.
- The board and leadership must agree to proceed.
- The organization should engage a third-party to conduct the study.
- Background research will be conducted on the organization, it's donor and volunteer base, and the community.
- Interviews are conducted by the third-party consultant.
- Findings are reviewed, and next steps are recommended.

Questions a Feasibility Study Should Answer for the Organization
- Is the capital campaign the correct strategy?
- Is the timing of the campaign optimal?
- Does the organization have the infrastructure to conduct a campaign?
- Who will lead the campaign? (both from a staff and volunteer standpoint)
- What is the constituent base's capacity and willingness to give?
- Is the constituent base ready and willing to support the campaign beyond financial gifts?

Common Fundraising Vehicles
- Direct marketing.
- Special events.
- Grant proposal writing.
- Corporate sponsorships.
- Cause-related marketing.
- Major gifts.
- Gift planning.
- Memorials.
- Membership and alumni program.
- Gaming & lottery programs.
- Workforce/payroll/federated campaigns.
- Peer-to-peer.

Measuring Tools to Evaluate the Success/Effectiveness of Fundraising:
- ROI (Return on Investment).
- Growth Rate (the growth in number of donors and money raised).
- Retention Rate (the number of donors who give subsequent gifts).
- Average Gift (online and offline).
- Average funds raised by volunteers (board members, peer-to-peer, etc.)
- Lifetime value of a donor.
- Cost per dollar raised.

Domain 3
Relationship Building
(29% of total scored items—51 items)

Introduction

Philanthropy comes as a result of meaningful relationships. As such, relationship building becomes a critical skill to master for any fundraising professional. Armed with proper fundraising research and a strong case for support (from domains one and two), relationship building becomes an easier function to perform as a development professional.

Recommended Reading

The publications on the Reading Resource List are all widely available and provide information on current, commonly accepted fundraising practices. These references have been identified as being the most comprehensive and most closely related to information covered on the examination.

It is not intended that each candidate read every publication on the Resource Reading List. Rather, this list is provided as a guide for candidates who are seeking sources of information on particular subject areas, or general overview texts. Reading any or all of the publications on this list does not guarantee you will do well on the examination.

- *The Fundraising Reader (2023)* by Beth Breeze, Pamela Wiepking, Donna Day Lafferty

- *Keep Your Donors (2008)* by Tom Ahern and Simone Joyaux

- *Beyond Fund Raising, 2nd Edition (2005)* by Kay Sprinkel Grace

- *Visual Planned Giving: An Introduction To The Law & Taxation Of Charitable Gift Planning* by Dr. Russell James III

- *Capital Campaigns: Strategies That Work 4th Edition (2016)* by Andrea Kihlstedt

- *Fundraising Basics: A Complete Guide: A Complete Guide 3rd Edition (2009)* by Barbara L. Ciconte and Jeanne Jacob

- *Fundraising Principles and Practice, 3rd Edition (2024)* by Adrian Sargeant, Jen Shang

- *Achieving Excellence in Fundraising 5th Edition (2022)* by Genevieve G. Shaker, Eugene R. Tempel, et al.

- *Fundraising for Social Change, 8th Edition* by Kim Klein, Stan Yogi

Key Terms & Concepts

Automated Clearing House (ACH) An electronic funds-transfer system that facilitates payments. It can be a way for organizations to accept donations from supporters who wish to give via direct debit. The automated clearing house processes "batches" of transactions and deposits funds into the organization's account.

Cause-Related Marketing An agreement that links a social cause with a product or service, with sales being divided in an agreed upon portion between the company and the organization.

Corporate Philanthropy Cash and in-kind gifts from a company to nonprofit organizations.

Communications Plan A comprehensive framework for how messages will be delivered, who will deliver them, and how they will be crafted. A policy-driven approach to providing information to internal and external sources to increase awareness, donor engagement and recognition, strengthen the case for support, and manage crisis communications.[30]

Development All of the aspects that encompass a fundraising program, including marketing and public relations.

Donor Recognition An organized policy and process of recognizing gifts. These include an immediate acknowledgement, subsequent personal expressions of thanks, and other methods.

Donor Relations Maintaining donor interest through organized communications, personal involvement, and acknowledgment.

Electronic Funds Transfer (EFT) A direct debit (usually monthly) from the donor's bank account to a nonprofit organization.

Gift Acknowledgement The process of thanking and recognizing the donor for their gift. It is typically done with a written acknowledgement or email for a gift made online. Larger size gifts may warrant a more personal acknowledgement. Timely gift acknowledgment within a 48-hour recommended period of time is a key component in donor retention and repeat giving.

Giving Club A segmented group of donors who give at regular intervals (monthly, annually) and receive special communications, access, and recognition based on membership.

LYBUNTS An acronym describing donors who made a gift "Last Year, But Not This" year.

Matching Gifts A highly effective tool to encourage others to give. Research has demonstrated that the likelihood of a gift increases 22 percent when a match is offered, and the revenue per solicitation increases 19 percent.[31] These may be matches offered by a donor or donors to the organization, a community foundation, or the organization itself.

Member Benefits Organizations that have a membership program typically create specific and exclusive benefits for participants. Examples include special access or priority seating at events, (subject to government limitations and guidelines), access to discounted services from partnering organizations, a membership card or car decal (alumni associations), name recognition in an annual report or member publication, donor wall, etc.

Naming Rights An agreement which outlines the mutual understanding between a donor and the organization about how the donor or donor's designee will be recognized and for how long with a named building, section of a building, program, event, position title, or other element. The agreement states the name to be used and other considerations.

Premiums An item or items of value given with a solicitation or promised as a result of a gift. Examples include personalized mailing labels or tote bags. After a decline in popularity in association with direct mail, these are making a comeback with crowdfunding campaigns and often incentivize giving.

Stewardship Plans An organizational plan for how gifts will be used in accordance with donor wishes and how that use will be reported back to the donor.

Unrestricted Gift A donation made to a charity for whatever use the organization determines.

Domain Content Review

To master the key concept areas of Relationship Building on the CFRE exam, a fundraising professional must be able to:

3.1 Initiate and strengthen relationships with constituents through systematic cultivation and stewardship plans designed to build trust in, and long-term commitment to, the organization.

3.2 Develop and implement a comprehensive communications plan to inform constituents about the organization, its mission, vision, values, financial and ethical practices, funding priorities, and the impact a donor can have by making a donation.

3.3 Create opportunities to position the donor(s) through their giving as part of the organization, its mission, aspirations, and vision.

3.4 Acknowledge and recognize donor gifts in ways that are meaningful to donors, appropriate to the mission, values, and policies of the organization, and in keeping with charitable laws.

3.5 Create a comprehensive strategy for engagement of constituents that leads to action with the organization.

Self-Assessment

Using the key term and concepts, the recommended reading materials at the beginning of this chapter, the *International Statement of Ethical Principles in Fundraising,* and the *Donor Bill of Rights*, assess your understanding of these key knowledge areas:

- Elements of a cultivation plan:

- Components of a comprehensive communications plan:

- Donor acquisition and renewal strategies:

- Communication methods, channels, and messages:

▶ Verbal and written communication techniques:

▶ Components and uses of active listening:

▶ Aspects of nonverbal communication such as body language and eye contact:

▶ Emotional intelligence:

▶ External spheres of influence such as corporate, governmental, social, civic, professional, religious, political, and cultural affiliations and their interrelationships:

▶ Methods for optimizing relationships between and among constituencies (for example, trust building or team building):

▸ Relationship between philanthropy and fundraising:

▸ Benefits of fundraising programs for organizations:

▸ Using incentives such as member benefits, special invitations, premiums, and naming rights:

▸ Stewardship techniques such as recognition and impact reporting:

▸ Definition of a culture of philanthropy:

▸ Charitable laws:

Study Questions

This section is meant to help you become familiar with the type of questions that you may encounter on the CFRE exam. Additional questions are found at the end of each knowledge domain chapter and in the CFRE Practice Exam.

Answers to the questions below can be found in Appendix II.

Questions

1. Which aspect of an organization's history is MOST often effectively used in appealing to donors?
   A. The external factors that impacted the organization.
   B. The identity of the organization's chief executive officers.
   C. The inauguration of various departments or new services.
   D. The role of major donors in developing the current strengths of the organization.

2. You have determined that donor retention should be a high priority moving forward. The BEST course of action to accomplish this is to:
   A. Recognize the donors publicly at events.
   B. Include the donors in upgrade efforts such as donor clubs.
   C. Invite new donors to contribute to other projects that need funds.
   D. Place the donors on the organization's mailing list.

3. As a general rule, what is the best way to cultivate major gifts?
   A. Appoint prospective donors to the board.
   B. Organize a series of events for prospective donors.
   C. Develop informed repeat donors.
   D. Think like an investor while developing the request.

4. When recognizing a major donor, it is most important for the fundraising professional to consider the:
   A. Donor's preference for recognition.
   B. Opportunities for publicity.
   C. Budget for high-quality recognition.
   D. Gift's significance to the organization.

5. Donors are most likely to not make a second gift when:
   A. They don't receive an annual gift summary in order to prepare their taxes.
   B. They are not thanked and informed about their gift's impact.
   C. They don't receive a thank you within 48 hours.
   D. They don't receive premiums with their gift.

Relationship Building Additional Review

Now that you have completed this chapter, outline any areas that will require more preparation and study:

Additional Best Practices

Notes on Corporate Giving
- Corporate giving over time has evolved. Companies are more focused on philanthropy that is productive and strategic.
- Corporate giving as a percentage of profits has gone down in the past 30 years, while cause marketing and sponsorships have gone up.
- Corporate giving now accounts for 5% of total giving.
- Of that total, 1/3 comes from corporate foundations.
- Companies are most interested in giving to causes that:
  - Create a link between the organization and company that is beneficial to the company socially and financially.
  - Are measurable, proactive, and focused.
- Ways in which companies support nonprofits:
  - Workplace charitable campaigns.
  - Direct gifts of cash.
  - In-kind gifts.
  - Volunteer projects.
  - Lending of experts/expertise.
- Motivations for companies to give:[32]
  - Improve the quality of life in the community in which they do business and their employees/customers live.
  - Improve the competitive environment in which they do business.
  - Attracting and keeping employees and customers.
  - Improving the quality and skills of their workforce.
- Methods of corporate funder research:
  - Annual reports.
  - Corporate citizenship and sustainability reports.
  - Volunteer (board member) connections.
  - LinkedIn.
- Four Models of Corporate Giving[33]
  - Corporate Productivity Model (Giving because it will help increase profits and boost stock value for shareholders).
  - Ethical or Altruistic Model (Giving because the company has an obligation to be a good corporate citizen and exhibit social responsibility).
  - Political Model (Giving because it secures, enhances, or protects corporate power and influence with government and community leaders).
  - Stakeholder Model (Giving because it is deemed the proper response to the needs of the various stakeholders who have an interest in the company. These include employees and their families, customers, the local community and organizations).
  - Understanding the four models will help the fundraising professional prepare the right solicitation plan.
  - Multiple models could be in play within the same organization at the same time.
- Cause Marketing vs. Sponsorships
  - Cause marketing is tied to the purchase of a product with a percentage of the proceeds going towards the nonprofit.
  - Sponsorships are not tied to purchasing behavior, but for a flat fee give the company visible marketing access to an event, cause, or activity.

Foundation Fundraising
- Foundation funding is often synonymous with proposal writing. However, the grant seeking process is comprehensive, and includes research, planning, and cultivation of relationships with foundation staff and leadership.
- Foundation giving is second only to individual giving in total philanthropic support.
- There are four types of foundations:
  - Independent Foundations: A private foundation that supports tax exempt organizations through grants.
  - Corporate Foundations: A foundation that functions like a private foundation, but receives its assets from the company it is associated with and prioritizes funding projects aligned with its business interests.
  - Community Foundation: A foundation that both makes and receives gifts and limits its funding to a specific geographic area.
  - Operating Foundation: A foundation that seldom makes gifts to other organizations, rather it is directly involved in the mission for which it was formed.
- Donor Advised Funds
  - Allows donors to make irrevocable gifts to a fund.
  - Allows donors to make future recommendations about future distribution of those funds.
  - Popular with donors who don't want to create their own foundation but want to have some control/influence on the destination of their grant funds.
  - May be located within a community foundation or a public grantmaking charity.
- Types of Foundation Support:
  - Operations (Unrestricted): Support ongoing operations with no use restrictions.
  - Program (Restricted): Support for a specific activity or plan.
  - Capital: Support for a building, facility expansion, equipment, or endowment.
  - Pilot: Support for a start-up program for a limited time.
  - Challenge: Support designed to encourage others to give to a campaign or project by matching the generosity of individual givers.

Components of a Comprehensive Communications Plan
- Determine a goal.
- Identify & profile audience.
- Develop messages.
- Select communications channels.
- Choose actives and materials.
- Implement the plan.
- Evaluate and begin again.

Donor Acquisition Strategies
- Use your donor management system to identify key segments and profile your "average" donor.
- Using these findings, identify unreached groups who have similar characteristics.
- Use a third-party company to perform research on prospective donors.
- Perform targeted outreach based on those findings.
- Vehicles for donor acquisition include:
  - Direct mail.
  - Telephone solicitation.
  - Social media.
  - Digital display ads and retargeting.
  - Email.
  - Search Engine Marketing (SEM).

Donor Retention Strategies
- Build a donor-focused approach to stewardship and cultivation.
- Provide excellent customer (donor) service.
- Follow-up in a timely manner.
- Communicate consistently.
- Provide evidence of value from the investment the donor has made.
- Follow-up with lapsed donors.
- Don't just ask them to give again. Give lapsed donors a platform to express their reasons for not continuing to give.
- Making giving convenient and encourage monthly giving.

Domain 4
Volunteer Involvement
(6% of total scored items—10 items)

Introduction

Volunteers are donors. They routinely give their time in support of an organization, and 80 percent give financially as well. On average, volunteers spend 36 percent of their time raising money for organizations while some organizations have even higher rates of volunteer-driven fundraising. Given this, it is not surprising that understanding how to recruit, manage, motivate, and properly thank volunteers is a critical piece in the life of a development professional.[34]

Recommended Reading

The publications on the Reading Resource List are all widely available and provide information on current, commonly accepted fundraising practices. These references have been identified as being the most comprehensive and most closely related to information covered on the examination.

It is not intended that each candidate read every publication on the Resource Reading List. Rather, this list is provided as a guide for candidates who are seeking sources of information on particular subject areas, or general overview texts. Reading any or all of the publications on this list does not guarantee you will do well on the examination.

- *The Fundraising Reader (2023)* by Beth Breeze, Pamela Wiepking, Donna Day Lafferty

- *Beyond Fund Raising, 2nd Edition (2005)* by Kay Sprinkel Grace

- *Visual Planned Giving: An Introduction To The Law & Taxation Of Charitable Gift Planning (2014)* by Dr. Russell James III

- *Capital Campaigns: Strategies That Work 4th Edition (2016)* by Andrea Kihlstedt

- *Fundraising Basics: A Complete Guide: A Complete Guide 3rd Edition (2009)* by Barbara L. Ciconte and Jeanne Jacob

- *Fundraising Principles and Practice, 3rd Edition (2024)* by Adrian Sargeant, Jen Shang

- *Achieving Excellence in Fundraising 5th Edition (2022)* by Genevieve G. Shaker, Eugene R. Tempel, et al.

- *Fundraising for Social Change, 8th Edition (2022)* by Kim Klein, Stan Yogi

Key Terms & Concepts

Advisory Board Provides some level of oversight and guidance to a nonprofit organization, but lacks the legal fiduciary obligations of a governing board. It is strategically comprised of individuals with influence, expertise, or prominence in the community.

Board of Directors Individuals selected in accordance with an organization's bylaws to oversee management, determine policy, and perform fiduciary obligations of an organization.

Budget A detailed description of income and expenses for an organization.

Campaign Leadership The volunteers who make up the core of a capital campaign's decision makers.

Governance The process by which a nonprofit board provides strategic leadership through vision casting, policy setting, strategic planning, oversight, and accountability.[35] Governance roles and structures are two key factors that prospective board volunteers review before making a decision to join and/or to give, as they are a reflection of "the character and quality of the institution."[36]

High Net Worth Volunteers Volunteers whose income and/or assets put them in a position to make substantial donations to an organization. In addition to the monetary contributions that high net worth individuals make, they often play strategic volunteer roles (such as board members or consultants) which are often based on their special skill set and experience. 75 percent of high net worth individuals who give to charity also volunteer.[37]

Organizational Readiness An assessment of an organization's level of resolve, capacity, and infrastructure necessary to accept and implement a significant change or project.

Roles & Responsibilities (Board) Can be broken down into four main aspects: adherence to legal obligations, adherence to mission, stewardship of resources, development.

Stewardship of Mission The responsibility of board and staff to ensure the viability of the organization.

Volunteer Diversity (For Boards) The process of selecting a board that demonstrates variety in viewpoints, ethnicity, gender, socioeconomic levels, age, etc.

Volunteer Orientation (For Boards) The process of acclimating board members to the organization, its culture, and their roles and expectations.

Volunteer Retention The rate at which board members remain committed to volunteering both during and after their terms end. Critical elements of successful retention include engagement, feedback, gratitude, acknowledgement, clear understanding of mission, and a sense of purpose.

Domain Content Review:

To master the key concept areas of Volunteer Involvement on the CFRE exam, a fundraising professional must be able to:

4.1 Assess organizational readiness to engage volunteers.
4.2 Create structured processes for the identification, recruitment, vetting, orientation, training, oversight, evaluation, recognition, retention, and succession of volunteers.
4.3 Develop role descriptions to empower and support volunteers and enhance their effectiveness.
4.4 Engage volunteers in various capacities (for example, board, program, campaign) in the fundraising process.
4.5 Participate in recruiting capable and representative volunteer leadership
4.6 Identify need and opportunities to engage volunteers.

Self-Assessment

Using the key term and concepts, the recommended reading materials at the beginning of this chapter, and the *Donor Bill of Rights*, assess your understanding of these key knowledge areas:

▶ Personality types and attributes:

▶ Volunteer roles in fundraising:

▶ Components and uses of volunteer role descriptions:

▶ Legal, regulatory, and organizational policy regarding volunteers:

▶ Strategies for optimizing volunteers' time and talent:

▸ Volunteer recruitment, orientation, vetting, training, management, motivation, retention, recognition, and evaluation techniques:

▸ Governance principles and models for not-for-profit organizations:

▸ Value of inclusion, diversity, equity, access, and community representation:

▸ Respective roles of board members and staff in governance and management:

▸ Trends in volunteerism:

▸ Organization's structure, functions, and culture:

Study Questions

This section is meant to help you become familiar with the type of questions that you may encounter on the CFRE exam. Additional questions are found at the end of each knowledge domain chapter and in the CFRE Practice Exam.

Answers to the questions below can be found in Appendix II.

Questions

1. You have decided to include volunteers in the fundraising process. However, since this hasn't been a priority, there is no structure for this to take place. To set it up, you should:
    A. Select members from your board and start to recruit them.
    B. Ask for interested persons to volunteer by publicizing the need.
    C. Ask the CEO to identify people, and immediately recruit the CEO's selections.
    D. Take the time to identify potential volunteers for the organization, and then recruit them.

2. Which of the following is the BEST volunteer recruitment source for a planned giving/bequest program?
    A. Clients and participants in past and current programs.
    B. Users of organizational services.
    C. Members, clients, and/or alumni.
    D. Board members, major donors, and financial professionals.

3. To maximize the outcome of working with volunteer leadership, it is most important for the staff to:
    A. Obtain a list of likely prospects from volunteers.
    B. Prepare a detailed job description for volunteers.
    C. Provide for effective use of volunteer time and skills.
    D. Present a strong case for support using volunteers.

4. How can volunteers be utilized to assess the giving potential of prospects?
    A. Ask volunteers to share their personal contacts.
    B. Ask volunteers to participate in the donor ranking process.
    C. Ask volunteers to make LinkedIn connections with high net worth colleagues..
    D. Ask volunteers to personally contact prospects and assess their giving capacity.

5. What are the key elements of a successful volunteer retention program?
    A. Training, vision casting, and frequent communications.
    B. Fundraising training, regular emails, and frequent opportunities to volunteer.
    C. Clear expectations, training, timely thank-yous, and regular communications.
    D. Clean and safe volunteer environment, food and drinks, and clear staff directions.

Volunteer Involvement Additional Review

Now that you have completed this chapter, outline any areas that will require more preparation and study:

Additional Best Practices

Volunteer Best Practices
- Keep volunteers engaged.
- State their roles clearly.
- Explain the benefits and outcomes of their roles and service.
- Don't waste their time.
- Always thank them for their time.
- Include volunteers in the planning process.
- Train volunteers in both their roles and the fundraising process.

Main Functions of a Volunteer Governing Board
- Define and embody the vision of the organization, set goals, and approve plans for reaching those goals.
- Approve, motivate, and support top administrative officers.
- Provide oversight and evaluate the effectiveness and performance of the organization and its top officers.
- Take action to maintain the organization's progress towards its mission, strategic plan, and fiduciary duties.

Roles and Responsibilities of Board Members
- Fiduciary duties: see that the organization is acting in the best interest of their constituents and using resources ethically.
- Legal duties (ensure an adherence to mission and bylaws, as well as to applicable laws)
- Review and approve major financial transactions.
- Fundraising.
- Strategic planning and vision casting.
- Serving as ambassadors and advocates.
- Contributing to the organization's culture.

Nonprofit Governance Best Practices
- Maintain corporate minutes of all board meetings and committee meetings that are authorized to act on behalf of the board.
- Annually review the conflicts of interest policy.
- Annually assess adherence to the conflicts of interest policy.
- Review and approve budgets and C-level compensation as prescribed in the organization's by-laws.
- Review and approve any reports that must be made to local, regional, and national government agencies.
- Maintain transparency to the public.

Methods by Which Board Members Support Fundraising[38]
- Making a personal gift.
- Participate in strategic planning/development plans.
- Identifying peers with the linkage, ability, and interest to give.
- Writing personal notes (solicitation letters or thank you letters).
- Introducing prospective donors to organization staff.

Recruiting Board Members

Recruiting board members mirrors fundraising efforts since the case for support is the rationale for extending the invitation. Additionally, the invitation implies an expectation for a philanthropic commitment to the organization.[39]

Recruitment efforts begin with a serious evaluation of board strengths and weaknesses. Consideration should be given to the role a prospective board member will play, their interest in the mission, and their likelihood of supporting the mission financially.

When meeting with a prospective board member in order to extend an offer, the meeting usually includes the following:

- Mission and case for support.
- An outline of the duties, responsibilities, and expectations of the member.
- The specific strengths the prospective member brings to the organization.

When recruiting board members and other volunteer leaders for a campaign, the following characteristics are necessary:

- Name recognition with groups served by the organization.
- A history of active involvement or association with the organization.
- A significant giving history with the organization.
- Connections with other leaders who represent the organization's constituencies.
- The ability and commitment to be active fundraisers.

The commitment and quality of board leadership is the most critical factor in determining the likelihood of a campaign's success.

Board Retention Best Practices
- Create a well thought out and strategic board orientation process.
- Give clear instructions on what you want the board member/volunteer to do.
- Run efficient meetings and events (don't waste their time).
- Optimize the agenda so members deal with key, high-level issues.
- Provide training and feedback regularly.
- Assign members to committees to keep them engaged.
- Match board member talents to staff needs (consider a staff/board mentorship program).
- Solicit board member input and feedback.
- Encourage and schedule social time with their peers before each meeting.
- Provide ample tools for members to raise funds and advocate on the organization's behalf.

In successful campaigns, contributions from the board and the foundation and companies they control range from 20 – 50% of the total amount raised.[40]

100% board participation in a campaign is the most powerful signal to prospective donors that the organization excels in carrying out its mission.

Solicitations by board members are most effective when they are:
- Peer-to-Peer (CEO to CEO for example).
- A friend or colleague.
- Conducted after careful research into the prospect's ability, linkage, and interest.
- Conducted after training the volunteer in the both the mission and case for support.

The Role of the Campaign Chair in a Capital Campaign:[41]
- Serving as CEO of the campaign.
- Presiding over steering committee meetings.
- Recruiting chairs for the subcommittees.
- Cultivating a small number of prospects (and soliciting them when the time is appropriate).
- Ensuring financial commitments from committee chairs.
- Working with the CEO/Chief Development Officer on planning, implementing, and marketing the campaign.
- Where appropriate, serving as campaign spokesperson in a variety of settings.

The Importance of Volunteers
- Volunteers give at double the rate of the general population that doesn't volunteer.
- 80% of volunteers give at least once per year.
- Households that volunteer give more than double the percentage of household income than those households that don't volunteer.
- The number one activity of volunteers is fundraising.
- Meeting attendance is not the sole gauge of a volunteer's worth or engagement.
- The right volunteer can have a significantly higher influence on a donor than development staff.
- It is the staff's responsibility to make the volunteer experience rewarding and enjoyable.
- Don't always ask volunteers to solicit donations. Instead, mix it up by asking them to send thank you letters.

Domain 5
Leadership and Management
(18% of total scored items—31 items)

Introduction

Leadership and management are core competencies of any development professional. Even when not in a management or supervisory role, development professionals are community leaders and are essential to helping a community understand and respond to needs.

As a fundraising professional, it is important to develop leadership skills and an understanding of the management functions that are necessary for working with the program teams and administration of an organization. It is also important to understand budgeting, forecasting, and strategic planning in addition to the skills needed to recruit, train, manage, and empower staff.

Recommended Reading

The publications on the Reading Resource List are all widely available and provide information on current, commonly accepted fundraising practices. These references have been identified as being the most comprehensive and most closely related to information covered on the examination.

It is not intended that each candidate read every publication on the Resource Reading List. Rather, this list is provided as a guide for candidates who are seeking sources of information on particular subject areas, or general overview texts. Reading any or all of the publications on this list does not guarantee you will do well on the examination.

- *The Fundraising Reader (2023)* by Beth Breeze, Pamela Wiepking, Donna Day Lafferty

- *Beyond Fund Raising, 2nd Edition (2005)* by Kay Sprinkel Grace

- *Fundraising Basics: A Complete Guide: A Complete Guide 3rd Edition (2009)* by Barbara L. Ciconte and Jeanne Jacob

- *Fundraising Principles and Practice, 3rd Edition (2024)* by Adrian Sargeant, Jen Shang

- *Achieving Excellence in Fundraising 5th Edition (2022)* by Genevieve G. Shaker, Eugene R. Tempel, et al.

- *Fundraising for Social Change, 8th Edition (2022)* by Kim Klein, Stan Yogi

Key Terms & Concepts

Annual Report A review of the revenue, expenditures, program results, and general state of the organization for the previous 12 months.

Cash Flow The amount of money being transferred in or out of an organization.

Constituency The broad population of people who have been or are currently involved with an organization, including supporters, volunteers, participants, recipients, staff, and leadership.

Data Integrity The accuracy and consistency of stored data. It is typically confirmed by the absence of discrepancies between two instances or updates of a data record.[42]

Development All of the encompassing elements of a continuing fundraising program (annual giving, special gifts, planned gifts, public relations).

Director of Development The individual responsible for leading the development (advancement and fundraising) efforts of an organization.

Elements of a Fundraising Plan Mission, goals, tactics, budget, and timeline. The mission should inform the goals for the upcoming plan, specifically what you want to accomplish and what time requirements and financial resources (budget) are required to accomplish those goals. Tactics include the types of fundraising to be used (annual giving, direct mail, events, corporate giving, etc.), and a timeline gives you a projection of how long it will take to meet your goals.

Feasibility Study An assessment of the fundraising potential of an organization, typically conducted by a third-party consultant. The results are usually submitted in report form with findings, recommendations, and plan.

Fundraising Counsel An individual or firm that advises nonprofit organizations in a variety of fundraising aspects.

GAAP Generally accepted accounting principles.

Gift Range Chart A chart of gifts that enables management to know, in advance of a campaign, the size and number of gifts necessary at each level of giving in order to achieve the campaign goal.

Market Research The process of gathering, organizing, and interpreting data regarding donor and prospective donor preferences, attitudes, interests, and giving ability.

Mission Statement A brief definition of the purpose of an organization, who it serves, and how it will carry out that service.

Performance Measurement The routine measurement of outcomes and results for a program or individual employee in order to compile the data needed to evaluate the impact and effectiveness of a program or employee. May include metrics such as number of contacts, number of proposals or solicitations, money raised, etc.

Strategic Planning A comprehensive process that identifies strategies that will position an organization to further its mission. The process often begins with a SWOT analysis which identifies an organization's strengths, weaknesses, opportunities, or threats. The process will usually result in either a reaffirmation of or adjustment to the mission, a definition of the internal and external context of the organization, and the creation of a set of definable and measurable objectives for the organization.

Vision Statement Defines the overall goals of an organization and what it aspires to look like in the future. It is a future-looking declaration of the organization's intended destination.

Domain Content Review

To master the key concept areas of Leadership and Management on the CFRE exam, a fundraising professional must be able to:

5.1 Demonstrate leadership that advances fundraising practice.

5.2 Advocate for and support a culture of philanthropy and the advancement of fundraising across the organization and its constituencies.

5.3 Ensure sound administrative and management policies and procedures are in place to support fundraising functions.

5.4 Participate in the organization's strategic planning process to ensure that fundraising and philanthropy are integrated within it.

5.5 Design and implement short- and long-term fundraising plans and budgets to support the organization's strategic goals.

5.6 Employ marketing and public relations principles and tools to support fundraising programs and organizational goals.

5.7 Conduct ongoing performance measurement and analysis of fundraising programs using accepted and appropriate standards and metrics to identify opportunities, resolve problems, measure against established goals, and inform future planning.

5.8 Recruit, train, and support staff and volunteers by applying human resource principles and best practices such as talent management techniques, on and off boarding of staff and volunteers, professional development, management, and leadership.

5.9 Utilize external services as needed to optimize the activities and outcomes of the fundraising function.

Self-Assessment

Using the key term and concepts, the recommended reading materials at the beginning of this chapter, the *International Statement of Ethical Principles in Fundraising*, and the *Donor Bill of Rights*, take a moment to assess your understanding of these key knowledge areas:

▶ Components and uses of mission, vision, and values statements:

▶ Strategic and action planning methods:

▶ Fundraising program evaluation standards, procedures, and methods:

▶ Policy and procedure development and evaluation:

▶ Elements of a fundraising plan:

▶ Role of fundraising in strategic planning:

▶ Organizational structures and team dynamics:

▶ Methods for ensuring the integrity and security of data:

▶ Components and uses of fundraising audits:

▶ Financial management including budgeting, financial statements, and audits:

▶ Elements and use of market research:

▶ Marketing and public relations principles:

▶ Methods for assessing organizational impact:

▶ Relevant professional development resources and requirements:

▶ Human resource management principles, strategies, and practices:

▶ Fundraising roles, job design, and structure:

▶ Characteristics of a culture of philanthropy:

- Methods to assess the need for external services or other resources:

- Techniques for selecting, evaluating, and managing external services:

- Principles and practices of managing meetings:

- Methods and strategies for managing change:

- Principles of effective leadership:

▶ Sources of historical and contemporary information about philanthropy and fundraising:

▶ Concepts of organizational development:

▶ Regulatory and legal issues related to management:

▶ Elements of inclusion, diversity, equity, and access:

Study Questions

This section is meant to help you become familiar with the type of questions that you may encounter on the CFRE exam. Additional questions are found at the end of each knowledge domain chapter and in the CFRE Practice Exam.

Answers to the questions below can be found in Appendix II.

Questions

1. An analysis of the basic data (participants, income, and expenses) from a direct mail solicitation has been completed. To determine the key performance measurements and effectively evaluate the direct mail program, you will need to examine the:
   A. Percent participation, average gift size, net income, average cost per gift, cost of fundraising, and return.
   B. Hierarchy of gifts as compared to gift total, and gift total as compared to rated potential.
   C. Budget income projections as compared to actual income from the direct mail program.
   D. Performance of this year's direct mail donors as compared to last year's donors who did not give this year.

2. Effective strategic planning for an organization must initially include:
   A. Hiring a consultant as the organization's planning process manager.
   B. Engaging key stakeholders in the planning process.
   C. Determining the organization's direction, mission, and vision.
   D. Conducting market research to assess potential opportunities.

3. The most common reason for straying from an organization's mission is:
   A. Overemphasis on the bottom line.
   B. Changing community needs.
   C. Deterioration of leadership.
   D. Trying to do too many things at once.

4. What metrics should be employed to measure the success of your fundraising efforts?
   A. Retention rate, giving frequency, and largest gift.
   B. Retention rate, average gift size, ROI, and percentage of goal achieved.
   C. ROI, cost per denomination of money raised, percentage of goals achieved.
   D. Largest gift, smallest gift, and median gift.

5. The elements of a successful fundraising plan include:
   A. A gift range chart, budget, organization chart, and monetary goal.
   B. Mission, goals, tactics, budget, and timeline.
   C. Goals, timeline, and budget
   D. Organizational chart, budget, and goals.

Leadership and Management Additional Review

Now that you have completed this chapter, outline any areas that will require more preparation and study:

Additional Best Practices

Budgeting (Capital Campaigns)

Elements to consider when determining the budget of a capital campaign:[43]
- Size of the goal.
- Method(s) of solicitation.
- Campaign method.
- Geographic reach of the campaign.
- Percentage of institutional resources committed to regular fundraising versus committed to the campaign.

A budget for conducting a capital campaign is typically 10-12 percent of the campaign goal itself (under $10 million) and 4 percent for a well-established organization with a goal of $25 million or more.[44]

Leadership Styles
- Positional: Leadership that comes with the job title.
- Tactical: Organized and decisive leadership to accomplish a goal. It is focused on balancing organizational needs with the needs of staff in order to gain desired results.
- Collaborative: Leadership that emphasizes shared ownership of the goal, assets, and results, and thus brings more people into decision-making roles in order to accomplish the organization's mission.

Budgeting
- The budget is a multi-year investment strategy for organizational resources.
- The budget implies a long-term growth strategy with a rate of return at minimum that exceeds US$1 per dollar invested and ideally realizes a rate of US$10-$20 per dollar invested.
- When creating a budget, essential questions to ask are:
    - What are the spending priorities as they relate to the mission?
    - What revenue is reasonably expected based on current organizational capacity and the philanthropic environment?
- Essential budgeting considerations, including:
    - Organization's mission and priorities.
    - Sources of revenue.
    - Gift projections (based on prior year revenues).
- Common evaluation terms:
    - CTRD: Cost to Raise a Dollar: A measure of efficiency that expresses the total amount spent to raise each dollar in support.
    - ROI (Return on Investment): A measure of fundraising effectiveness. It represents the return on each dollar spent.
    - Net Return: Gross fundraising revenue minus gross fundraising expenses.

Marketing and Communications for Fundraising
- Exchange is at the heart of mutually beneficial relationships (between people, organizations, governments, etc.).
- Marketing facilitates and assists in the exchange process.
- For a nonprofit, marketing should be an organizational mindset. Each member should consider the organization from an outsider's perspective.
- Marketing, for a nonprofit, centers on three specific areas:
  - Analyzing the market in which the organization conducts activities.
  - Establishing goals, objectives, strategies, and tactics by which the organization will deliver its message to its constituencies.
  - Creating and managing a budget and system of evaluation of marketing goals and outcomes.
- Methods of Market Research
  - Quantitative.
  - Qualitative.

Elements of a Fundraising Plan

The following components are necessary to create and execute a fundraising plan:
- Case for support.
- Needs statement.
- Internal & external research (SWOT analysis, market research, focus groups, donor giving history & trends, etc.).
- Organizational strategic plan.
- Organizational budget.
- Determination of fundraising vehicles.
- Donor database.
- Stewardship plan.
- Organizational chart with assigned roles for staff and volunteers.

Measuring Organizational Impact
- Nonprofits make an impact on their communities both in the short- and long-term. Often long-term impacts are harder to measure and define.
- Typically, funders want to see the most measurable impact of support and that is usually defined by outcomes.
- Outcomes should be articulated in specific terms, defining what took place, over what span of time, and what change was made to/for the target community or participants.

Human Resources Best Practices[45]
- Provide Security to Employees: This includes both workplace safety and employment security and is an essential component in staff retention.
- Hire the Right People: Find people with the best combination of ability, trainability, and commitment.
- Self-Managed Effective Teams: The organization should create an environment where teams thrive, are encouraged to share ideas, and work well with other teams.
- Fair and Performance-Based Compensation: Using a mix of organizational performance rewards along with individual performance rewards keeps individuals motivated to maximize their own salary outcomes while encouraging a sense of ownership in the outcomes of the organization.
- Provide Relevant Skills Training: Budget for and encourage both relevant skills training and life-long learning.
- Creating a Flat & Egalitarian Organization: Organizations should uphold the value of all members of the team and consider policies that emphasize equal respect.
- Make Information Easily Accessible: Open communication projects trust and enhances morale. It also promotes efficiency and cooperation between teams.

Organizational Development Concepts
- Organizational development is the application of behavioral science to help organizations improve systems, teams, and individuals.
- The primary goal is to help people function better within the context of the nonprofit organization.
- It seeks to align human behavior with that of the organization's mission and goals.
- The lines between human resources and organizational development are often blurred. However, OD tends to function at a higher level than employee engagement and seeks to improve the total system and outcomes both inside and outside the walls of the organization.

The Role of Fundraising in the Strategic Planning Process
- The strategic plan helps clarify the direction the organization will go in pursuit of its mission.
- The strategic plan will also define what steps the organization will take to execute its philanthropic goals.
- Fundraising exists to serve those philanthropic goals, not as an end to keep the doors open.
- Fundraising is a management function and should be regarded as such in both the strategic plan and in the leadership structure of the organization.
- Development staff are critical to the strategic planning process. Input from development should include:
    - Historic fundraising results.
    - Realistic goal setting and revenue expectations.
    - Growth and cultivation strategies.
    - Leadership and vision casting.

Domain 6
Ethics, Accountability, and Professionalism
(10% of total scored items—18 items)

Introduction

Trust is the foundation for all philanthropy. Development professionals are held to a high standard of professionalism and accountability because nonprofit organizations are stewards of the public trust. A breach of this trust can cause irreparable harm to an organization, and even a community. The nature of soliciting gifts and building relationships calls for the recognition of, adherence to, and modeling of a code of conduct based on ethics and professionalism.

Recommended Reading

The publications on the Reading Resource List are all widely available and provide information on current, commonly accepted fundraising practices. These references have been identified as being the most comprehensive and most closely related to information covered on the examination.

It is not intended that each candidate read every publication on the Resource Reading List. Rather, this list is provided as a guide for candidates who are seeking sources of information on particular subject areas, or general overview texts. Reading any or all of the publications on this list does not guarantee you will do well on the examination.

- *The Fundraising Reader (2023)* by Beth Breeze, Pamela Wiepking, Donna Day Lafferty

- *Keep Your Donors (2008)* by Tom Ahern and Simone Joyaux

- *Fundraising Basics: A Complete Guide: A Complete Guide 3rd Edition (2009)* by Barbara L. Ciconte and Jeanne Jacob

- *Fundraising Principles and Practice, 3rd Edition (2024)* by Adrian Sargeant, Jen Shang

- *Achieving Excellence in Fundraising 5th Edition (2022)* by Genevieve G. Shaker, Eugene R. Tempel, et al.

- *Fundraising for Social Change, 8th Edition* by Kim Klein, Stan Yogi

Key Terms & Concepts

Accountability "An obligation or willingness to accept responsibility or to account for one's actions."[47] In nonprofit terms, accountability is the process of opening oneself and the organization to scrutiny, voluntary external review, and feedback from stakeholders. In 1995, the Association of Fundraising Professionals adopted the following definition of accountable organizations: "The accountable organization clearly states its mission and purpose, articulates the needs of those being served, explains how its programs work, how much they cost, and what benefits they produce. The accountable organization freely and accurately shares information about its governance, finances, and operations. It is open and inclusive in its procedures, processes, and programs consistent with its mission and purpose."[48]

Annual Report The most common tool used to exhibit transparency and detail stewardship. Typically produced at the end of the fiscal year for the organization, it is a comprehensive report of all revenue and expenses. Additionally, it shows how the organization used the resources it received in order to advance its mission and explain how successful those efforts were.

Audit An evaluation of fundraising procedures, policies, and results by an organization, usually conducted by a third-party entity.

Consultant A fundraising specialist hired by an organization to recommend solutions to problems, provide advice, and offer guidance.

Charitable Deduction The value of a gift of cash, securities, or property transferred to a legally recognized charitable organization, deductible for income, gift, and estate tax purposes. Typically, this refers to the portion of a gift that is deductible from the donor's income subject to federal income tax.

Conflict of Interest A situation in which a person in a position of trust is faced with competing professional and personal interests.[49]

Donor Intent A donor's expectation of how a gift will be used and what outcomes may be expected from the use of the gift are defined as donor intent. Donor intent is the guiding principle for how gifts should be accepted and used. All efforts should be made to honor donor intent regardless if the gift is restricted or unrestricted—even unrestricted gifts have the implied purpose of furthering the organization's mission. If donor intent does not align with the mission and policies of the organization, this should be discussed with the donor. If an agreement cannot be reached, the gift should not be accepted. In other words, if the organization cannot carry out the donor's wishes as intended, the organization should not accept the gift.

Donor Recognition The creation and implementation of a system of recording and thanking donors that is accurate and timely. This process is critical to both transparency and donor retention. Donors must be acknowledged and thanked in ways that are meaningful and appropriate to the gift level. Donors are best served when gift acknowledgements express the value of the investment the donor has made and its impact on the mission of the organization.

Appropriate gift acknowledgement creates the proper environment for future communications between the donor and the organization. Some items to consider:

1. Review the legal requirements of your region to determine your organization's obligations for receipts and disclosures.
2. Organizations should have a written policy for recording, recognizing, and acknowledging gifts, and it should be reviewed on a regular basis.
3. Ensure that gifts are recorded accurately in a secure database.
4. In general, donors should be thanked within 48 hours of making a gift.
5. Gift acknowledgements can be and often are separate from receipts. These are more personal in nature and stress both the benefit to the organization's mission and the gratitude of the organization.
6. Include a contact person in the acknowledgement for the donor to contact should they have questions about their gift or the organization. This may or may not be the signatory.

Key Terms & Concepts continued

Donor Records One element of donor trust is that the organization will be a good steward of donor's gift and the donor's information. Implied in that trust is that the organization will not misuse or share the donor's information without prior consent. The donor should also be able to expect that the organization will take all reasonable measures to ensure the safety of digital information from being compromised via a data breach. Privacy and security policies should be in place and reviewed regularly.

It is also important to know how your state, region, or territory defines a data breach (what information is included/excluded) and what are the reporting requirements in the event one occurs. Should your organization carry data liability insurance or is it required where you operate? Finally, what will be your response to donors and other stakeholders if a breach occurs?

Donor information and the permission implied with it is our single greatest asset as development professionals. As such, it should be treated with great care. Donor records should be kept clean and updated with a high priority on accuracy. Records should include but are not limited to:

1. Full name and salutation.
2. Address.
3. Email address.
4. Giving history (with dates, amounts, and related donor appeals).
5. Volunteer history (where applicable).
6. Preferred method(s) of communication.
7. Preferred method(s) of giving.
8. Event participation (where applicable).
9. Appeals sent/received (via all forms of communication).
10. Donor relationships (to staff, to the board, to other volunteers/donors).

Ethical Fundraising The sum total of applying transparency, accountability, and the Donor Bill of Rights to all aspects of fundraising. The ethical fundraising professional does not seek personal gain, but rather puts the donor first and the organization second in all fundraising activities.

Fiduciary Duty The legal obligation to act on behalf of another or others with resources that have been entrusted.

Gift Acceptance Policy A best practice that establishes what types of gifts your organization is willing to accept and provides an explanation for donors on what is acceptable. It may also be a requirement, based on your region or country's laws.

The gift acceptance policy is an effective tool for managing the expectations of your donors. While some gifts may be in opposition to the organization's mission or values, other gifts (commercial real estate, for example) may be beyond the organization's ability or resources to accept and maintain. In either case, the gift acceptance policy helps guide the conversation between the perspective donor and development professional.

Some considerations for the policy include:

1. Include the advice of legal counsel with language in the policy for donors to seek professional counsel.
2. Be clear and specific about types of gifts that will not be accepted.
3. Spell out any specific arrangements such as special acknowledgements and/or naming rights, as well as terms and conditions for removing names from organizations or physical space.
4. Distribute the policy to the development team, executive staff, and board members.
5. Share the policy on the organization's website.
6. Determine who will review the policy and how often the review will occur.[50]

Key Terms & Concepts continued

Gift Instruments The legal vehicles that define how and when a gift will be transferred and used (sometimes called a gift agreement). In addition to the gift acceptance policy, there will be times when a gift necessitates a gift agreement. For most gifts to a nonprofit, the implied agreement is that the organization will use the gift in pursuit of its mission or specifically directed to a certain project if that was the intent of the gift.

However, when a large or complex gift requires a trust or agency arrangements, the organization and the donor will enter into a gift agreement that spells out the terms and conditions of the gift. These types of gifts could include securities, real estate, appreciated works of art, or gifts that provide donors with certain tax benefits.

Common Elements of Gift Instruments:

This list is neither comprehensive nor is it a substitute for securing legal advice before entering into an agreement.

- Date of the agreement.
- Legal name(s) of the donor and recipient.
- Detailed description of what is being contributed and the dates on which it will be contributed and the amount (cash) or quantity (personal property assets) or legal description (private or commercial real estate).
- Description of the means of transfer and instrument(s) of conveyance, where applicable.
- The purpose for which, and time periods during which, the gift may be expended.
- Determination that the donor's gift or pledge is unconditional and irrevocable, and that the designation of the organization as recipient also is irrevocable.
- Whether the gift is irrevocable, but the donor retains the right to amend the recipient. In such a case, the contribution would be conditional and not recordable by the organization.
- A statement of the donor's intent in the event that the donor passes before execution of the gift agreement.
- Any other terms, restrictions, or other details agreed-to by the organization and the donor(s).
- A definition of purposes for which the gift may not be used by the organization.
- The signatures of an authorized representative of the donor and organization.[51]

Legal Standards Prevailing local and regional laws and rules that determine how gifts are solicited and used.

It is incumbent upon the fundraising professional to understand the legal implications of fundraising both where you operate and where you raise money as the laws and rules may be different where your organization is headquartered from those regulations in other countries. Do you raise funds online? Do your disclosures and policies apply to a donor who does not reside in your territory? *The exam will not ask country-specific questions, but it is important to know for your own practice and the well-being of the organization you serve.*

Mission Statement The articulation of the purpose of an organization, including who it serves, the implied community need, and how the organization meets that need.

Professional Development Ongoing training and learning for the development professional. The fundraising professional has a duty to pursue continuous education, understanding, and mastery of best practices within the field to stay on top of changes in the law that impact fundraising, and be mindful of new technologies and resources as they emerge.

It is important to grow in understanding of the best practices within the field as well as becoming well-rounded citizens. Fundraising professionals are encouraged to seek opportunities such as professional organization membership, mentorship, research, committee involvement, and sources of continuing education.

Key Terms & Concepts continued

Professional Mentoring The practice of advising or training a younger or less experienced colleague. Organizations (such as Association of Fundraising Professionals, Canadian Association of Gift Planners, Association of Healthcare Philanthropy, etc.) offer you a professional community in which to grow, seek mentors, become a mentor yourself, and to learn. Such organizations also have a code of conduct or ethics that members must adhere to which also promotes ethical best practices.

Professional Standards Accepted best practices and ethical codes of conduct of a sector. In the nonprofit sector, those professional standards are best expressed in the Donor Bill of Rights, International Statement of Ethical Principles in Fundraising, and member organization documents like the Association of Fundraising Professionals Ethical Principles and Standards, the Association of Healthcare Philanthropy Professional Standards and Conduct, etc.

Public Trust Public trust (in a nonprofit context) refers to an organization created for the benefit of the community or to meet societal needs. Nonprofits enjoy a unique status as tax exempt organizations. In return for that status and the benefits implied, the organization is expected to be ethical and transparent in its efforts to address the community need inherent in its stated mission. This is the essence of the concept of public trust and implies that nonprofit organizations and their employees are held to a higher standard of conduct than those operating in a different sector.

Stewardship The process of accepting and managing resources that have been entrusted to the organization through philanthropy. Good stewardship culminates in reporting to donors that funds were used as intended and the results of that use. Tasks that are typically associated with good stewardship include but are not limited to:
- Honoring donor intent.
- Maintaining accurate and secure donor records.
- Reporting on both restricted and unrestricted gifts.
- Keeping donors apprised of endowment results.
- Timely execution of annual reports and all government required reporting.[52]

Transparency The process of allowing the public access to information that sheds light on an organization's stewardship of gifts, program outcomes, and daily operations.

Domain Content Review

To master the key concept areas of Ethics, Accountability, and Professionalism on the CFRE exam, a fundraising professional must:

6.1 Ensure all fundraising activities and policies comply with ethical principles and legal standards.
6.2 Communicate principles of ethical fundraising to stakeholders to promote ethical practices and strengthen a culture of philanthropy.
6.3 Promote ethical fundraising as a crucial component of philanthropy to strengthen the non-profit sector and support the sector's role as a pillar of civil society.
6.4 Honor donors' intent by clarifying, implementing, and monitoring instructions regarding the use of gifts.
6.5 Ensure allocations of donations are accurately documented in the organization's records.
6.6 Report to constituents the sources, uses, impact, and management of donations to demonstrate transparency and enhance public trust in the organization. When donors' intent cannot be fulfilled, proactively communicate with donors and mutually agree on a shared solution.
6.7 Participate as an active and contributing member of the fundraising profession through activities such as mentoring, continuing education, research, and membership in professional associations.
6.8 Ensure all fundraising activities and policies align with the values of the organization.

Self-Assessment

Using the key terms and concepts, the recommended reading materials at the beginning of this chapter, the *International Statement of Ethical Principles in Fundraising*, and the *Donor Bill of Rights*, take a moment to assess your understanding of these key knowledge areas:

▶ Laws and regulations relevant to not-for-profit organizations:

▶ Legal and ethical practices related to donor record maintenance, gift accounting, financial management, and audit trails:

▶ Methods of recording, receipting, recognizing, and acknowledging gifts:

▶ Elements of gift acceptance and recognition policies:

▶ Elements of gift agreements:

▶ Accounting and investment principles for not-for-profit organizations:

▶ Organizational transparency, such as methods for reporting fundraising performance, outcomes, and impact to constituencies:

- Donor rights and codes of ethics for fundraising professionals:

- Protection of personal privacy and information:

- Ethical principles relevant to cultivating, securing, and accepting gifts:

- Methods and processes for ethical decision making:

- Professional development and practice leadership opportunities in fundraising:

▶ Mentorship principles:

▶ Resources to support advocacy for fundraising practice:

▶ Appropriate avenues for advocacy:

▶ Elements of organizational policies:

Study Questions

This section is meant to help you become familiar with the type of questions that you may encounter on the CFRE exam. Additional questions are found at the end of each knowledge domain chapter and in the CFRE Practice Exam.

Answers to the questions below can be found in Appendix II.

Questions

1. What role does donor intent play in deciding how to use a gift of property?
   - A. The donor is always right. Use the gift in the manner they prescribe.
   - B. Donor intent should be balanced against the needs of the organization.
   - C. Ultimately, the fact that it is a gift implies that the organization can decide how best to use the property.
   - D. Donor intent should be honored as long as it does not violate your gift acceptance policy.

2. How soon should donors be thanked for their gifts?
   - A. Immediately upon receipt.
   - B. Within 48 hours.
   - C. Within 3-5 business days.
   - D. All donors can be thanked on the 15th and 30th of the month.

3. When visiting a senior donor in a nursing home, should a family member be present?
   - A. If one is available, include a family member. If not, include staff.
   - B. If the donor is mentally sound, a family member is not required.
   - C. Yes, a family member should be present any time you visit a donor in a nursing home.
   - D. If a gift is being discussed or agreed upon, then a family witness or power of attorney must be present.

4. Should a gift be accepted from a corporation whose CEO is under indictment?
   - A. No, it could embarrass the organization.
   - B. If the property is not connected to the indictment and it does not violate the organization's gift acceptance policy, it is okay to accept the property.
   - C. Yes. If it will help the organization, the source is not relevant.
   - D. Yes, if the property can then be sold quickly.

5. What should be included in a gift acceptance policy?
   - A. Definition of acceptable gifts, recording and acknowledgement procedures, privacy procedures, and when to refuse a gift.
   - B. Conflicts of interest, naming rights, and how to solicit matching gifts.
   - C. Gift annuity rates, tax language, and donor research procedures.
   - D. Stock transfer procedures, board member giving expectations, and employee giving enrollment.

Ethics, Accountability, and Professionalism Additional Review

Now that you have completed this chapter, outline any areas that will require more preparation and study:

Additional Best Practices

Stewardship
- Stewardship is a process that begins even before accepting an initial gift. It starts with the establishment (by the board) of policies that define how an organization will accept, process, and invest gifts.[53]
- Stewardship is an ongoing process of saying thank you, expressing appreciation, giving attention, providing information, and welcoming feedback.

Principles of Ethical Fundraising
- Ethics go hand-in-hand with the execution of fiduciary duty and stewardship.
- Fundraising professionals should always act in the best interests of the organization, while recognizing donor intent.
- Organizations should seek to avoid the appearance of impropriety.
- Ethical fundraising includes using discernment to differentiate between a gift made for philanthropic purposes and a gift made for influence and/or access.
- Organizations that raise money must have a gift acceptance policy in place and it should be reviewed by fundraising staff on a regular basis.
- Fundraising professionals have a duty to report to their CEO or board any potential conflicts of interest.
- Ethical fundraising includes a commitment to transparency in regard to stewardship, reporting, and strategic planning.
- Ethical fundraising requires adherence to the tenets of the *Donor Bill of Rights* (see Section 2).
- Ethical fundraising comes with an implication that the organization or individual fundraising professional will take all reasonable steps to protect donor privacy and information.
- Fundraising professionals will not share donor contact information (selling or renting lists) without disclosure of intent to do so.
- Except as required by law, donors should have the right to determine the limits of the information they provide to an organization and the extent of that information that may be made public.
- Organizations have the responsibility to define how information will be collected, used, shared, and protected.

Donor Recognition, Receipting, and Recording Best Practices
- Gift acknowledgements should be made within 48 hours of the gift.
- Additional recognition of the gift should be made in accordance with the organizations' gift acceptance policy.
- A donor's wishes to remain anonymous must be upheld.
- The process of donor cultivation should include learning any cultural or religious views on gift acknowledgement (e.g., some cultures take offense to public acknowledgement of charitable giving).
- Consult local/regional/national regulations on the detail, timeline, and contents of the receipt.
- Centralize the collection of gift information and record keeping.
- Use the receipt process as an opportunity to reinforce the mission and the organization's gratitude for the gift.
- It is common to send an acknowledgment separate from the receipt. These are typically more personal and don't necessarily have to come from the centralized office (typically sent from the gift officer involved).
- Create an acknowledgement process to govern the initial stewardship of a gift. It should include but not be limited to:
    - Timing of the thank you.
    - Customization.
    - Signatories.
    - Levels of acknowledgement.
    - Memorial procedures.
    - Delivery methods and responsibilities.
    - Recording procedures.
    - Internal communications expectations and procedures.

Memorials and Honorific Gifts
- Follow the same procedures in place for receipting and recognizing regular gifts.
- In addition, there will be two acknowledgements: one for the donor and one for the family of the honoree.
- Create clear and simple instructions for how a person can make such a gift.
- Establish who in the family of the honoree should receive the notifications.
- Include donor contact info in the report so the family can thank the donor.
- Include in the donor acknowledgement that the family will be notified.
- When possible, indicate familiarity with the person honored and the appropriateness of the tribute.
- When possible, work with the family to produce a statement as to why the organization was important to the honoree.

Gift Restrictions
- Major and legacy gift donors sometimes insist on restrictions of use for part or all of their donation.
- Accepting these types of gifts must first be made in accordance with the organization's gift acceptance policy.

Examples of Gifts That Should Not Be Accepted or Should Be Returned
- Any gift where the money was obtained by illegal activity.
- Any gift where the donor maintains interest in the use of the funds. (e.g., endowing a chair to a university and then insisting on naming the chair).[54]
- Any gift that would constitute an assault on the integrity of the organization if it were to be accepted.
- Donations from a vendor with the expectation of future business from the nonprofit organization.
- Any gift that would create a conflict of interest or violate the organization's gift acceptance policy.

Gift Acceptance Policies
A gift acceptance policy should include, but not be limited to, the following:
- A definition of acceptable gifts.
- An explanation of the circumstances by which the organization will accept or reject a gift.
- Expectations for staff regarding stewardship, donor intent, and donor privacy.
- Donor recognition guidelines.
- Any local/regional/national legal requirements.
- Instructions/procedures for a change of circumstances and how those will be communicated to the donor.

Ethical Principles for Making the Ask[55]
The following ethical principles have been adopted by AFP International as well as other international fundraising organizations:
- Honesty: Protect the public trust by acting truthfully at all times.
- Respect: Conduct all fundraising activities with respect to the dignity of the profession and the donors.
- Integrity: Avoid the appearance of impropriety and avoid conflicts of interest.
- Empathy: Promote a culture of giving, ethical standards, individual privacy, and freedom of choice.
- Transparency: Provide clear information about fundraising activities and results.

Transparency Best Practices
- Transparency can be defined as sharing accurate and true information about your organization, its partnerships and affiliations, your mission, and goals.
- Post required disclosures (tax form and other reports) as dictated by your local/regional/or national government.
- Share an annual report that conveys sound fiscal policy and execution, income and expense proportionality, and that resources are resulting in community impact.
- Create a culture of transparency among staff, volunteers, and leadership.
- Utilize the organization's website as a tool for displaying transparency. Make it easy for people to answer the questions: What do you do? And what do you do with my gift?

The Benefits of Transparency
- Engagement: Donors stay engaged longer and make a deeper commitment to organizations that prioritize transparency.
- Donations: Organizations viewed as highly transparent receive 53 percent more in revenue than those perceived as not transparent.
- Donor Relationships: Donor retention is higher with organizations that are perceived to be transparent.
- Engagement: Donors stay engaged longer and make a deeper commitment to organizations that prioritize transparency.
- Donations: Organizations viewed as highly transparent receive 53 percent more in revenue than those perceived as not transparent.[56]
- Donor Relationships: Donor retention is higher with organizations that are perceived to be transparent.[57]

Section Four

Test-Taking Strategies for the CFRE Exam

Even experienced, knowledgeable fundraising professionals sometimes worry about taking the CFRE exam. This is understandable and natural—after all, most of us have little experience of taking exams after finishing formal academic studies. To help you get back into a test-taking mindset, we'll first share some information about the CFRE exam so that you know how it is developed. We'll then get into some question-answering strategies that you can practice and use once the day comes when you take the CFRE exam.

Where Do CFRE Exam Questions Come From?

As attested by the CFRE certification program's accreditation by the ANSI National Accreditation Board (ANAB) under globally accepted ISO/IEC 17024 standards for certification of persons, CFRE International follows best-practice standards in the development and administration of the CFRE certification program. A number of rigorous steps are followed continuously to assure the CFRE is psychometrically valid and of the highest quality.

CFRE International works with a professional testing agency that performs detailed analysis of all CFRE exam questions as well as the CFRE exam as a whole. The CFRE International Exam Committee, the members of which are all current CFREs, write and validate contents of the exam questions.

The following steps are part of the test development process used in creating the CFRE exam:

- **JOB ANALYSIS:** A comprehensive research study that is conducted every five years to validate contemporary fundraising practice. The Job Analysis surveys fundraising professionals around the globe regarding the tasks they perform in their work, how often they perform those tasks, the importance of the tasks to fundraising success, and the knowledge used to perform the tasks. Results are compiled by the professional testing agency and validated by members of CFRE International's Job Analysis Task Force, the members of which are all current CFREs.
- **TEST CONTENT OUTLINE:** The CFRE Test Content Outline describes the body of fundraising knowledge tested by the CFRE exam. The Test Content Outline is derived directly from the results of the Job Analysis.
- **ITEM (TEST QUESTION) DEVELOPMENT AND VALIDATION:** The CFRE International Exam Committee, who are all current CFREs and represent a cross-field of philanthropic organizations and world regions, are trained to write items (test questions) for the CFRE exam. Once written, items are reviewed by Exam Committee working groups to ensure accuracy of content and clarity of expression.
- **PRE-TESTING:** The CFRE exam contains 200 questions. Of these, 175 count toward the candidate's score. All questions on the exam that affect a candidate's score have been pre-tested to make sure they are statistically valid and that there are no flaws in question construction. The 25 questions on the CFRE exam that do not affect the candidate's score are being pre-tested for potential use in a future exam.
- **EXAM FORM CREATION AND REVIEW:** Under the direction of professional psychometricians, the CFRE International Exam Committee creates a draft exam of 200 items that matches the blueprint of the CFRE Test Content Outline. During this process, the draft is reviewed to identify overlap or overemphasis of certain topics prior to being approved for use as the CFRE exam.

- **PASS POINT STUDY:** A panel of current CFREs goes through a process facilitated by professional psychometricians to identify the minimum number of questions a candidate will need to answer correctly to show mastery. This minimum number constitutes the raw score that a candidate must achieve in order to pass the CFRE exam. The psychometricians then convert the raw score to a normed scale where 200 is the lowest score possible, 800 is the highest score, and 500 is the minimum score that must be achieved to pass the CFRE exam. (This normed scale is commonly used by high-stakes exams.)
- **KEY VERIFICATION:** A final check of the answer key for the CFRE exam is conducted to assure that the correct answers are accurately indicated.
- **EXAM ADMINISTRATION:** Candidates take the CFRE exam.
- **ONGOING EXAM REVIEW:** Statistics on individual test questions and on the CFRE exam as a whole are monitored annually. Unexpected results are brought to the attention of the CFRE International Exam Committee for review and action, if necessary.

What Are CFRE Exam Questions Actually Based On?

Exam questions are based on what fundraising professionals do every day, but are framed against the broader context of professional knowledge that has been tested and measured within the international fundraising community and that is considered ethical best practice. The practical application of this is that correct answers on the CFRE exam reflect generally accepted principles of best practices in ethical fundraising. The actual, day-to-day practices you observe at your organization may or may not consistently reflect these generally accepted best practice principles.

CFRE International's Job Analysis research study collects and details the actual day-to-day skills, tasks, and critical levels of understanding and task applications for fundraising professionals in each of the six knowledge domains of fundraising. Each CFRE exam question is both rooted in one of the knowledge domains and is referred to in at least one (preferably two) specific and commonly accepted books that support the best answer.

Only those tasks performed most frequently or deemed most critical by the majority of Job Analysis respondents are included on the CFRE exam. This means the CFRE exam covers a broad base of fundraising knowledge. Candidates with a great deal of knowledge in one focused area will still need to have some familiarity with other areas of fundraising. Likewise, candidates need not feel they should be experts in every type of fundraising.

The Structure of CFRE Exam Questions

The CFRE exam uses a multiple-choice question format which is the "gold standard" of the certification industry and the most objective and reliable indicator for measuring mastery of a broad range of professional subject matter. Each question tests something found within the CFRE Test Content Outline.

The multiple-choice questions on the CFRE exam have three parts:
- **STEM:** The question that needs to be answered.
- **KEY:** The answer choice that is the correct answer to the question.
- **DISTRACTORS:** The answer choices that are incorrect answers to the question.

Some questions on the CFRE exam are short, while others are longer and provide more information or present a situation. Some questions are complete statements that end with a question mark. Others are incomplete statements ending with a colon (:), with answer options being possible completion of the sentence.

Each question in the CFRE exam has four possible answer choices (one key and three distractors). There is only one best correct answer for each test question. Some candidates look for information not contained in the question and think, "Well, the answer depends on this or that." This is not the case. All information needed to answer the question is presented to candidates. There are no "trick" questions. CFRE exam questions are based on best practices in ethical fundraising and are supported by professional literature. There is only one most correct answer.

Some further information regarding incorrect answer options (distractors): these answers are not designed to "fool" the candidate. They are designed to act as plausible but incorrect answers that the knowledgeable candidate must be able to distinguish from the information in the correct answer.

Strategies for Taking the CFRE Exam

Success in answering multiple-choice questions—including those on the CFRE exam—requires subject matter knowledge, but it also helps if you are an effective test-taker. To improve your success in answering multiple-choice questions correctly, use these strategies for answering multiple-choice questions:

- Read questions carefully. Read all the answer choices all the way through. Do not stop reading as soon as you believe you have found the correct answer. You might ignore an answer which more precisely answers the question being asked.
- Trust your first impression or "gut instinct." There is a correct answer to each question. It is widely believed that your first impression of the correct answer will be a better choice.
- Avoid overanalyzing. Focus simply on what is being asked. All the information needed to answer the question is in the stem. One mistake often made by candidates is reading too much into the question or making assumptions that go outside the question.
- Try to identify the answer before reading the choices. After reading the question, think of what answer you expect to find. Then read the choices. By doing this, the correct answer is more likely to jump out at you.
- Pick out key words and/or information. When reading the stem, notice any key points of information, such as type of fundraising or desired outcome. Note any key words, data, or terms which may affect the answer. Review the key information provided in the stem. What may be the correct answer in one circumstance many not be in another, given what is provided to you in the question.
- Avoid viewing the questions as having too little information. The information provided in the stem and your own recall of facts and reasoning ability should be sufficient to answer the question. Of course, if you were presented in real life with the situation posed in the question, you might well desire additional information, which could affect your answer, but this is not given in the stem. View the question as it is presented. What is the best practice answer, given the information presented in the stem?
- If uncertain, mark the question and return to it later. If you cannot decide quickly on an answer, mark it for review and return to it later. Go through the exam answering what you know first. Skip over more difficult questions and go back to them later.
- Eliminate obvious distractors. For most questions, there are usually two distractors (options) that usually appear to be incorrect; one that is plausible but incorrect; and one correct answer. When you first read the question, try to eliminate two of the answers first. If you cannot decide between the remaining two, make the question for review and come back to the question later.
- Make an educated guess. To improve your guessing ability, the first step is to eliminate any of the possible choices which you know, or are reasonably sure, are incorrect. Eliminating one or more of the possible choices improves your chance of selecting the correct choice. When guessing among four options, you have a 25% chance of getting it right; eliminate one option and your chance of guessing correctly is one in three and increase to 33%. If you can reasonably eliminate two of the options, your chance of guessing correctly increases to 50%.

- Don't worry about what you don't know. If you don't know the answer to a question, don't let it rattle you and affect your outlook on the other questions. Make an educated guess and move on.
- Limit the time you are spending on each question so you can complete the entire exam. If you are spending more than 30 seconds thinking about an item, skip it and go on to the next one.
- Check your answers. Once you have gone through the entire exam, go back and work on the questions you did not answer. Check your time periodically. Again, do not spend too much time agonizing over one item. Inevitably, there will be some questions you cannot answer.
- Don't worry about the exam. Many people feel drained and inadequate after taking a long exam. That feeling is not necessarily related to doing poorly on the exam.
- Go home and celebrate having completed this journey. Documenting your professional experience, studying, and taking an exam are tremendous accomplishments that you should be proud of.

Sample Questions with Answer Rationales

Answer these sample questions, analyze why the right answer is correct, and why the wrong answers are incorrect. Answer rationales for each option are provided so you can practice getting into a test-taking mindset.

Question 1

The first step in developing a strategy for approaching prospective donors for a gift is to:
A. Research the characteristics of current donors.
B. Evaluate results of former campaigns.
C. Use direct mail to attract repeat donors.
D. Set goals, strategies, and priorities.

Answer & Rationale for Question 1

The correct answer is A.
By researching the characteristics of current donors, an organization can develop a profile of their donors and identify those likely to give to your organization. Researching your current donors will provide insight into their motivations for giving, identify their interest in your organization's mission, and is helpful in discovering the common characteristics they share. Knowing this information is the first step in developing strategies for gift solicitations.

Answer B is not correct.
Evaluating results of former campaigns, while helpful for identifying giving trends, will not provide knowledge to an individual's motivation for giving.

Answer C is not correct.
Using direct mail to attract repeat donors is one of several fundraising vehicles that can be used for soliciting gifts. To select an appropriate fundraising vehicle, however, you must first know your donors' characteristics.

Answer D is not correct.
Similarly, to set goals, strategies and priorities, it is first necessary to have sufficient information about your donors; by researching the characteristics of current donors.

Question 2

When a donor wishes to make a planned gift/bequest/legacy gift to the endowment fund, the fundraising officer should first:
A. Offer to contact the donor's financial organization and advisor.
B. Explore what the donor wishes to accomplish with the gift.
C. Identify and share with the donor the organization's future needs.
D. Introduce the donor to various planned giving options.

Answer & Rationale for Question 2

The correct answer is B.
Fundraising officers that are successful in raising major gifts recognize their role as helping prospective donors fulfill their goals and aspirations in making a gift. Thus, answer B is correct; the first step in this scenario is to discover what the donor wishes to accomplish with the gift.

Answer A is not correct.
Contacting the donor's financial advisor or organization may be helpful later in the gift process, if the donor deems it appropriate, but it is not the first step. In many cases, the donor wants to personally consult with the advisor and does not wish the fundraising officer involved at all.

Answer C is not correct.
While the fundraising officer may have many needs of the organization to share with the donor, the first step is not to sell the organization's needs but to first determine what the donor wants. It is most important to focus on the donor's needs first.

Answer D is not correct.
Unless the fundraising officer first understands the donor's needs and wishes, it would be premature to share planned giving/bequest options. These are usually developed after understanding the donor's needs and financial situation.

Question 3

Market segmentation is best defined as:
A. Geographical boundaries where the services are offered.
B. Submarkets or segments of the public.
C. Determination of services for specific public sectors.
D. Segmenting the public by age groups.

Answer & Rationale for Question 3

The correct answer is B.
Market segmentation is dividing your constituencies into distinct subgroups, each of which has something in common, thereby allowing you to target those you want to reach.

Answer A is not correct.
It is not correct, since it deals with the institution's services, determining which services to offer to specific sectors and where they are offered, rather than segmenting constituencies into subgroups.

Answer C is not correct.
For the same reasons as A, C is not correct, since it also deals with the institution's services and determining which services to offer to specific sectors, rather than segmenting an organization's constituents.

Answer D is not correct.
Since it describes one way of dividing the market but does not define what market segmentation is.

Question 4

Before beginning to write the case for support for an upcoming campaign, it is MOST important to:
A. Acquire an understanding of the various donor target markets.
B. Budget an adequate amount for design, writing, printing, and dissemination.
C. Obtain an outline approved by the key people of the organization.
D. Design the piece with the other current organizational printed material in mind.

Answer & Rationale for Question 4

The correct answer is A.
Professional fundraising is based on relationship building. Without acquiring a basic understanding of the target markets being approached, valuable time and effort may be misdirected or ineffective. The case for support speaks to the organization's key target audiences and its preparation logically begins with the acquisition of a better understanding of what the interests, predispositions, and motivations within these markets might be when it comes to making a gift to your cause. By using valid market information to develop your case statement, you will be more successful in your appeals.

Answer B is not correct.
Understanding your target markets precedes writing. Writing and editing necessarily precedes design and production. While circumstance might require you to budget unknown costs for writing and production in advance, answer A is inherently more important than answer B in the context of developing a case for support for an upcoming campaign.

Answer C is not correct.
This information may be helpful in compiling the organization's own goals and directions, but does not necessarily reflect the views and expectations of the target donors you hope to approach. Targeted donor information needs to be acquired objectively and directly.

Answer D is not correct.
The design and production of the printed piece can proceed only after its content has been written. Designing it to fit other existing printed materials may or may not be suitable depending on its content, originality, desired impact, overlapping target audiences, etc.

Additional Sample Exam Questions

If you're looking for additional sample exam questions, please see Appendix II. The CFRE Practice Exam is another resource for additional sample exam questions.

Section Five

Preparing for and Taking the Exam

There is much to consider in the time leading up to and following your CFRE exam. This section provides information to help you know what to expect as you prepare for success.

BEFORE THE CFRE EXAM

Taking a certification exam is a major event in your personal and professional life, so you will want to prepare yourself appropriately through careful study and preparation. Equally important as your confidence about the exam's content is your confidence in your approach to the exam.

For most adults, it has been some time since they last took a standardized exam or test of any kind. The prospect of having to demonstrate professional knowledge used on a daily basis in an exam format may raise anxieties. You may be anxious, but you've got the experience and you've planned for this!

Preparing Yourself for the Exam

As a certifying agency, CFRE International adheres to international standards for the development and operation of a certification program.

These standards state that the same organization which assesses candidates cannot also prepare them for the exam. Therefore, in order for the certification process to be fair and reliable, CFRE International cannot sponsor or endorse any review or preparation courses.

CFRE International provides its participating organizations with the Test Content Outline and encourages those organizations to offer educational programming that covers topics found on the exam. However, each participating organization is the sole determiner of the content of its review courses and the quality of the instruction provided. The CFRE Exam Compass course is the only CFRE exam preparation curriculum developed by CFRE International. Members of the CFRE International Exam Committee (who are solely responsible for CFRE exam content) and CFRE International staff members supporting the work of the Exam Committee do not advise on the CFRE Exam Compass curriculum.

Because the CFRE exam is a generalist test based on current best practices in ethical philanthropic fundraising practice, any educational activities in which you participate from a reliable provider are going to assist you in mastering the knowledge and skills you need to be successful on the CFRE exam.

Some candidates may choose to participate in informal or structured courses, which are intended to prepare candidates for the CFRE exam. Typically, these are conducted by local chapters of professional associations related to fundraising, or by universities or private agencies. The length and cost of such preparatory courses vary widely.

Other resources you may consider as you prepare include the CFRE Recommended Resource Reading List (see Appendix I) and the CFRE Practice Exam.

For a sample study plan, see Section 6.

Scheduling Your Exam

The CFRE exam is administered by Pearson VUE and its partners. CFRE International will provide you with information for scheduling your exam with Pearson VUE once your CFRE application is approved. Please schedule your testing appointment with Pearson VUE as soon as possible to ensure the most convenient location, date, and time for your appointment.

- The CFRE exam is available worldwide at Pearson VUE Authorized Test Centers. You will be able to select the available center of your choice when you schedule your appointment with Pearson VUE through its website or call center.
- Most testing centers are open Monday through Saturday and many have evening hours. The test duration is four (4) hours, with additional time for a computer tutorial before the test begins. You will be making your own personal testing reservation and may be testing with people from a variety of different professions.

Appointment Scheduling Procedures

1. Log in to your account at My CFRE (https://cfre.secure.force.com) on the CFRE International website to verify your name and contact information.
   - Your first and last name, as entered in your contact information at My CFRE, must match your valid (i.e., not expired) government-issued photo identification document (ID) such as a driver's license or passport).
   - Your contact information will be used for all subsequent correspondence from CFRE, including sending your certificate when you pass.
2. The following information is needed to schedule your exam online with Pearson VUE:
   - A valid e mail address (for receiving your testing appointment confirmation).
   - Email received from Pearson VUE with account information.
   - Your name as listed on your government-issued photo ID.
   - Name of the Examination Sponsor: CFRE International.
   - Your daytime telephone number.
3. Go to the Pearson VUE website (www.pearsonvue.com/cfre) to schedule your appointment.
   - Select "Sign In" and follow the instructions. You must sign in as a Returning User using the login and password provided by Pearson VUE via email.
   - You will be able to obtain driving directions and a map from the scheduling page. Pearson VUE Technology Centers are located near convenient parking.

If necessary, you may also schedule by telephoning Pearson VUE Customer Service. Phone numbers for your region can be located on the Pearson VUE website at www.pearsonvue.com/cfre/contact.

In the United States and Canada, operators are available Monday through Friday from 7:00 AM to 7:00 PM Central Time (US). Outside of this region, operators are available Monday through Friday from 9:00 AM to 6:00 PM in local time. If scheduling by phone, please determine your preferred testing center location using the Pearson VUE website before scheduling the testing appointment.

Confirming Your Appointment

- When you register with Pearson VUE, you will receive an email with your appointment details and confirmation number. Please print a hard copy of your confirmation for your records.
- It is the candidate's responsibility to verify that the correct date, time, and place have been requested.

Cancelling and Rescheduling Appointments

Authorized candidates will only be able to choose a date within the testing window selected during Step 4 of the application. To request a new testing window, please contact CFRE for an Authorization to Test (ATT) Reissue Form. The form and associated ATT Reissue Fee must be returned to CFRE before your authorization can be updated.

If you need to cancel or reschedule your testing appointment within the same window, you must take one of the following steps:
- Sign in to your account on the Pearson VUE website (www.pearsonvue.com/cfre).
- Contact Pearson VUE Customer Service (www.pearsonvue.com/cfre/contact).
- For either method, please have your appointment confirmation number available.

All appointments cancelled less than forty-eight (48) hours prior to the exam will forfeit the full exam fee and be required to obtain a new eligibility.

Candidates who fail to cancel their appointment within the required forty-eight (48) hours and do not follow the above stated policy will need to submit a request in writing to be moved to a new testing window and pay both the ATT Letter Validity Fee and the Computer-Based Testing Fee.

Please contact the CFRE International Certification office for complete details of this policy.

Problems with Pearson VUE Scheduling

If you have difficulty scheduling your appointment with Pearson VUE, please email CFRE International at succeed@cfre.org or call CFRE International during normal business hours, 9:00 AM – 5:00 PM EST at +1 703 820 5555.

The Day Before and Day of the CFRE Exam

One of the most effective ways to prepare for an exam is to be certain you are feeling confident both physically and mentally. It is recommended that you get a good night's sleep the night before the exam and try to relax the evening before. A brief content review is fine, but the night before the exam is not the time to do late-night intensive cramming. You want to go into the exam feeling refreshed and ready to concentrate.

A bit of planning in the days before the exam can go a long way toward feeling confident and avoiding problems which can be unsettling the day of the exam. If travel is required to your testing center, consider staying close to the exam location the night before. If the location is unfamiliar to you, obtain directions from the testing center website. You may want to consider visiting the exam location a few days ahead of time. Determine where you will park and if you will need to bring money to pay for parking.

Wearing comfortable clothing during the exam is also important. Exam rooms may have temperature conditions that differ from the local weather, so dressing in layers is best. In cooler weather, the room may be especially warm; during the summer months, air conditioning may be turned up very high. Layers of clothing which you can add or remove as you adjust to the room environment are recommended.

Plan to eat something before the exam as it will be several hours before you have the chance to eat again. Food and drink are not permitted in the testing area, although some sites may have vending machines available. All sites do have water coolers. You will be permitted to leave the room to get a drink or use the restroom as needed, but the clock will not stop during breaks.

On the Day of the Examination:

- Bring two forms of identification (one government-issued) with at least one bearing your signature and photo, as signature-bearing, photo identification is required for admittance to the exam. These should be valid forms and not expired. If you do not bring it, the proctor will not admit you. The name on your identification must exactly match your ATT letter.

  Do not plan to bring any books, calculators, papers, or reading materials as these items will not be permitted in the exam room. You will be given scratch paper or a dry erase board on which to make any notes.

- Be punctual – arrive on time. Your testing confirmation will state at what time you should arrive. When you arrive, you will need to go through the admissions process. If there are many candidates at your exam site, this may take some time.

- Once you have checked in, you will be required to leave all handbags and other personal belonging in a secure locker. You will not be permitted to bring anything into the exam room, including food and drink. If you require the use of durable medical equipment (i.e., cane, insulin pump) during the exam, please notify CFRE International BEFORE you take the exam so CFRE International can alert the testing center. Otherwise, you may not be permitted to take the medical equipment into the secure testing area.

- Once admitted, you will be escorted to your seat and the proctor will log you into the exam. Please be sure to verify that you have received the correct exam before you proceed. Call any discrepancy to the attention of the proctor immediately.

- You will then have the opportunity to take a brief tutorial to orient you to the computer screen and show you how to navigate through the exam. Time spent on the tutorial is not part of the four (4) hours you have to complete the exam.

- Once you begin the timed portion of the exam, you have four (4) hours to complete it.

- When you have finished your exam and submitted it, you will be taken to a short survey about your test-taking experience.

- There is a 10 minute break after the first 100 questions. You won't be able to go back to those first 100 after your break, but you can mark and go back to them <u>before</u> the break.

- In addition to being available at Pearson VUE's global network of testing centers, the CFRE exam can come to you. With Pearson VUE's secure online proctoring platform, OnVUE, you can now sit for the exam from the comfort of your home or office. Visit cfre.org/remote-proctoring-for-the-cfre-exam/ for more details.

Section Six

After the CFRE Exam

As you leave the testing room, candidates will receive their score reports immediately upon completion of the exam.

Upon receiving a copy of your scores, CFRE International will mail you your final certification determination. If you have been successful on the exam, you will receive your official certification letter and a certificate that is suitable for framing at the end of the test window. If you were not successful, you will receive further instruction as to your options for proceeding.

How is the CFRE examination scored?

CFRE International is committed to offering a written exam that is comprehensive, that tests current fundraising practice, and is valid and reliable. To that end, CFRE International continuously reviews and revises the CFRE examination. A new form of the exam is released every 12 months.

There are several series of reviews, checks, and balances to ensure candidates are given the best and fairest examination possible. Several groups of current CFREs around the world volunteer their time to work with CFRE International's professional testing agency to assure a fair and credible examination.

CFRE International works with Pearson VUE to monitor the performance of each individual test question. Despite all the checks and reviews, there are occasions when an individual test question performs differently in an actual testing situation than what was expected. If it appears that the question was misleading or had more than one correct answer, CFRE International may opt to allow more than one answer to be accepted as correct or might score the question correct for everyone. This way, no candidate is unfairly penalized for a flaw in test construction.

CFRE International reports its scores as a scaled score. Scaled scores for the CFRE exam range between 200 and 800, with 500 being the passing point. A score of 800 represents a perfect score. The candidate's "raw score" (the actual number of questions answered correctly) is converted to the scaled score. This statistical procedure provides a common scale for reviewing and reporting results.

All candidates receive a score report that shows them the overall scaled score required to successfully pass the exam (and also provides the candidate with a breakdown by content area of their exam performance).

Candidates receiving a scaled score of 500 or greater will have successfully met the minimum for passing the examination. Those with a scaled score of 499 or less will not have met the minimum standard for passing the examination.

CFRE International uses a "criterion-referenced" exam model. As such, they may be different from "norm-referenced" exams that are typical of other exams you may have taken.
"Norm-referenced" exams are those that are graded on a curve. This means the candidate's performance is evaluated in relationship to others taking the examination. This is not the case with the CFRE examination. CFRE International does not pre-determine the number of candidates who will pass the exam.

The passing point for the examination, a scaled score of 500, has been set in advance using a panel of currently certified CFREs as subject matter experts. These subject matter experts are guided by CFRE International's professional testing agency in determining a psychometrically sound passing point for the CFRE exam.

The passing point for the exam will not change from exam administration to administration. It will not change from exam to exam. Your score will not be dependent on any one else with whom you are testing.

When will I get my examination results?

After you take the CFRE examination, you will receive test results (pass/fail) at the testing center.

Upon receiving your scores from the professional testing agency, CFRE International will confirm you your final certification determination. If you have been successful on the exam, you will receive your official certification letter and a certificate that is suitable for framing. If you were not successful, you will receive further instruction as to your options for proceeding.

If You Don't Pass The Exam

Once your application is submitted, it is valid for a 12-month period. Candidates who do not pass the exam are eligible for two (2) re-exam attempts per application. There is a fee to retake the exam, and you must wait thirty (30) days before taking the exam again. At the end of 12 months, you must submit a new application and pay the full application fee.

Application Requirements For Recertification

Once initial certification is awarded, CFREs must recertify every three years to maintain the CFRE credential. The recertification application works on a point system and requires candidates to document information in three categories: Education, Professional Practice, and Professional Performance. Candidates must document a minimum number of points in each of the three categories in order to be recertified. Your online application at My CFRE will automatically calculate points for you. Candidates must also reconfirm their commitment to ethical fundraising. Providing you maintain your credential by recertifying every three years, you do not have to take the CFRE exam again.

Section Seven

Creating Your Personal Study Plan

There isn't a set number of hours to study for the CFRE exam that will guarantee you a passing score. Everyone's background is different, which means how long everyone needs to study will be different.

On average, people who successfully pass the CFRE exam have studied at least 40 hours. If you have been in fundraising for fewer than five years, you will likely need to study longer as the exam is written at the five-year practice level.

Following the steps below is not a guarantee of a passing score on the CFRE Exam. But the steps may help you in being confident in structuring a systematic review of the content you wish to cover as you prepare for the CFRE Exam.

Step 1: Determine what you need to study

- Print and review the Test Content Outline.
- Underline any bullet points you are unfamiliar with, have not encountered yet in your career, or do not feel confident you could answer test questions about. Alternatively, you may prefer to test your knowledge with the CFRE Practice Exam (US$59.95 for 30 days unlimited access/$99.95 for 90 days unlimited access). Note: The CFRE Practice Exam is not required to successfully prepare for the CFRE Exam.

Step 2: Determine the resources you will use

We have identified the books on the Resource Reading List to be the best ones to help prepare you properly for the exam. Reading books not on this list as part of your preparation may not provide you with adequate information you need to pass.

- If you noticed the bullet points you underlined on the Test Content Outline are clustered into a few Knowledge Domains, visit the Resource Reading List to see the books that will help you best understand those areas.
- If the bullet points you underlined are fairly evenly distributed across the six Key Knowledge Domains, you may find it more helpful to read generalist books from the Resource Reading List that address multiple Key Knowledge Domains.

Many libraries and local foundation centers stock these books or will order them upon request. You may also want to ask your employer to purchase them and start a small staff lending library. If you know a CFRE, you may want to check if they have any books they used to study that they would be happy to lend you.

Step 3: Create your study plan

Decide if you will use an 8- or 16-week study plan. You may wish to use a shorter or longer timeframe depending on work and personal commitments.

Plan to take written notes as you study (do not rely solely on highlighting passages) to fully absorb the content. Make flashcards to break down complex pieces of information as well as to help you recall newly-learned best practices.

REMEMBER: The CFRE Exam tests how well you know best practices and can navigate real-world scenarios. It is not about rote memorization of facts.

Below is an 8-week study plan. This may easily be modified into a 16-week study plan by taking two weeks to cover each area outlined below.

- **Week 1:**
    - Skim the key terms in the knowledge domain sections of the CFRE Study Guide so you are familiar with the language of the exam. Also review the International Statement of Ethical Principles in Fundraising and the Donor Bill of Rights and think about the ways in which fundraising best practice is grounded in ethics.
    - Study the Current and Prospective Donor Research Knowledge Domain.
- **Week 2:**
    - Study the Securing the Gift Knowledge Domain.
- **Week 3:**
    - Study the Relationship Building Knowledge Domain.
- **Week 4:**
    - Study the Volunteer involvement Knowledge Domain.
- **Week 5:**
    - Study the Leadership and Management Knowledge Domain.
- **Week 6:**
    - Study the Ethics, Accountability, and Professionalism Domain.
- **Week 7:**
    - Re-read all your notes. Test yourself with the flashcards you have made. Re-print the Test Content Outline and underline any areas with which you still feel unfamiliar. Plan to re-read book passages to address these gaps in knowledge during this week.
- **Week 8:**
    - Review any areas you have had the least professional experience with and test yourself again with the flashcards.
- **The day before the exam**
    - Many people take off from work the day before the exam to review notes. This is not the time to cram. The benefit of taking the day off is that you won't run the risk of working late the night before your exam and/or feel drained from a hectic day at work.
    - Review selected key terms as well as your notes and flashcards one last time. Get a full night's rest and think positive thoughts. With all of the studying you've done, you should feel confident and prepared.

Exam Knowledge Domains	Number	Percentage of exam
Current and Prospective Donor Research	28 Items	15%
Securing the Gift	46 Items	22%
Relationship Building	52 Items	29%
Volunteer Involvement	16 Items	6%
Leadership and Management	38 Items	18%
Ethics, Accountability, and Professionalism	20 Items	10%

Study tips

- Don't study at home if easily distracted there.
- Many CFREs tell us they studied on their lunch break in their office.
- Using flashcards? Have your friends, family, children, or roommates quiz you.
- If you have children, study while they're doing homework.
- Set yourself a goal each week for how many pages you will read (be sure to stick to it!).
- Find a study group or start your own.
- Watch The *CFRE Exam: Setting Yourself Up for Success* (approx. 60 minutes)
- Leave your phone in another room while studying.

Section Eight

You've Passed Your CFRE Exam! Hurray! – What Happens Next...?

You've read, studied, and just completed your CFRE exam. The message is right there on your computer screen at the testing center—you passed!

After all the work, study, and worry that went into achieving this career milestone, you're feeling a well-deserved sense of pride in your accomplishment. Congratulations! You're a CFRE!
You also may be wondering, what happens next?

Within 24 hours of passing your exam, Pearson VUE will send your score to the CFRE International office. We will then update your account with the information that you passed. Then:

- The update of your online account triggers an email to you that your CFRE certification has been officially awarded.
- Within 5 business days, your name will be added to the Find A CFRE look-up resource on the CFRE website. (http://www.cfre.org/find-a-cfre/)
- Add the CFRE credential and the accompanying CFRE digital badge to your business cards, print and digital signature blocks, stationery, social media account profiles, and any other place your name is listed for business purposes. In fact, we encourage you to do this as it helps expand the recognition of the credential across the philanthropic sector. Style: John (or Jane) Q. Fundraiser, CFRE
- An online PDF press release, customized to your accomplishment as a new CFRE, is made available on the My CFRE page of your online account on the CFRE website. The "View My Press Release" hyperlink is located to the right of My Applications Summary. Use this press release to share your accomplishment with the leadership of your organization, announce it on your organization's website, and/or distribute it to local press in your community.
- Look for opportunities to talk about your CFRE credential, the rigorous process involved in achieving it, and what it demonstrates about you and others who hold the credentials as fundraisers.
- Log in to your account and begin your new Recertification Application. Even though recertification is three years away, starting early allows you to use the application as an easy, online tool to organize and track the new continuing education credits you'll be accumulating. When it comes time to submit your recertification application, you'll appreciate that you've been entering these items as you achieved them.
- Within 15 business days following the closing date of the testing window in which you passed the CFRE exam, CFRE International will mail you the hard copy of your CFRE certificate, which is suitable for framing.

Congratulations and welcome to the Certified Fund Raising Executive community, a global network of leaders in philanthropic fundraising who demonstrate their commitment to confidence, ethics, and professionalism in fundraising. Be proud that you are now a champion for professionalism in fundraising and share your commitment with others by encouraging them to start on the journey to becoming a CFRE.

Stay plugged in. Visit our website often and join the conversation on social media by following us on Facebook, Twitter, and LinkedIn, or by participating in CFRE Central, our online community.

APPENDICES

Appendix I

CFRE Recommended Resource Reading List

Many fundraising professionals ask for suggested publications to read to prepare them for the examination. In studying for your CFRE exam, you will probably seek out some resource materials and other references to read.

The publications on the Reading Resource List are all widely available and provide information on current, commonly accepted fundraising practices. These references have been identified as being the most comprehensive and most closely related to information covered on the examination.

It is not intended that each candidate read every publication on the Resource Reading List. Rather, this list is provided as a guide for candidates who are seeking sources of information on particular subject areas, or general overview texts. Reading any or all of the publications on this list does not guarantee you will do well on the exam.

While this reference list is provided by CFRE International and each exam item is drawn from facts that can be substantiated by professional texts, the exam is not intended to be an assessment of your knowledge of literature. Additionally, there is no single reference, or small group of references, that are associated with most of the questions on any given exam form. The best advice is to review a basic, widely-used reference. You may then wish to seek additional information not covered in that publication.

Please note that CFRE International periodically updates the CFRE Recommended Resource Reading List. While we have included the most recent list as of the date of publication of this Study Guide, you may wish to view the on-line CFRE Recommended Resource Reading List. The online list will contain any updates that have happened since the publication of this Study Guide.

Complete Reading Resource List

Each of these resources covers one or more of the six Knowledge Domains of the CFRE exam. Knowledge Domain Codes contained in the table are the following:

KD1 = Current and Prospective Donor Research
KD2 = Securing the Gift
KD3 = Relationship Building
KD4 = Volunteer Involvement
KD5 = Leadership and Management
KD6 = Ethics and Accountability

You can use Knowledge Domain Codes in the table search function to find books for Knowledge Domains. For example, if you want titles on Securing the Gift, enter "KD2" in the search box. If you want titles that cover more than one domain, enter more than one Knowledge Domain Code. For example, if you want titles on Securing the Gift and Volunteer Involvement, enter "KD2 KD4"

Title	Knowledge Domains Addressed
Keep Your Donors (2008) by Tom Ahern and Simone Joyaux	KD1, KD2, KD3, KD6
Beyond Fund Raising (2nd Edition) (2005) by Kay Sprinkel Grace	KD1, KD2, KD3, KD4, KD5
Visual Planned Giving: An Introduction To The Law & Taxation Of Charitable Gift Planning (2014) by Dr. Russell James III	KD1, KD2, KD3, KD4
Capital Campaigns: Strategies That Work (4th Edition) (2016) by Andrea Kihlstedt	KD1, KD2, KD3, KD4
The Fundraising Reader (2023) by Beth Breeze, Pamela Wiepking, Donna Day Lafferty	KD2, KD3, KD4, KD5, KD6
Fundraising Basics: A Complete Guide: A Complete Guide (3rd Edition) (2009) by Barbara L. Ciconte and Jeanne Jacob	COMPREHENSIVE KD1, KD2, KD3, KD4, KD5, DK6
Fundraising Principles and Practice, (3rd Edition) (2024) by Adrian Sargeant, Jen Shang	COMPREHENSIVE KD1, KD2, KD3, KD4, KD5, KD6
Achieving Excellence in Fundraising (5thEdition) (2022) by Genevieve G. Shaker, Eugene R. Tempel, et al.	COMPREHENSIVE KD1, KD2, KD3, KD4, KD5, KD6
Fundraising for Social Change, (8th Edition) (2022) by Kim Klein, Stan Yogi	COMPREHENSIVE KD1, KD2, KD3, KD4, KD5, KD6

APPENDIX II

Questions and Answers

Domain 1: Current & Prospective Donor Research:

1. In setting up a fundraising program focused on foundations for a new organization, the FIRST step is to:
    A. Make appointments for key volunteers to meet with foundation board members.
    B. Make an appointment for the chief executive officer to meet with foundation heads.
    C. Call on all foundations previously dealt with to let them know of the new cause.
    D. Research foundations that give to similar organization, and follow up.
    ANSWER: D

2. The primary purpose of rating an organization's donors is to determine their:
    A. Interest in the organization's cause.
    B. Involvement in the organization.
    C. Willingness to give to the organization.
    D. Potential to give to the organization.
    ANSWER: D

3. The process of establishing the financial range of gifts that a donor will reasonably consider is referred to as:
    A. Rating.
    B. Determination.
    C. Research.
    D. Cultivating.
    ANSWER: A

4. Foundation prospects for an organization are best identified by the geographic scope of the foundation, its granting criteria, and the foundation's:
    A. Board.
    B. Previous giving history.
    C. Most recent award.
    D. Capacity for grants.
    ANSWER: B

5. Prospective donors for an organization are best identified by:
    A. Apparent philanthropic interest.
    B. The organization's past and current board members.
    C. Interest in the organization's services.
    D. Links with the organization, giving ability, and interest.
    ANSWER: D

Domain 2: Securing the Gift

1. In preparation of the case statement, which of the following important pieces of information should be included first?
    A. Specific objectives and goals of the organisation.
    B. Mission statement of the organisation.
    C. Environmental issues affecting the organisation.
    D. Specific problems and needs addressed by the organisation.
    ANSWER: B

2. What considerations must be made when accepting a non-cash gift (securities, property, etc.)?
    A. The likelihood of the property being sold for cash.
    B. The value of the gift and tax implications of accepting it.
    C. The gift's appropriateness relative to the organization's gift acceptance policy.
    D. The timing of the gift relative to the annual campaign.
    ANSWER: C

3. Who are the key stakeholders that should be involved in developing a case for support?
    A. The CEO, the board chair, and the development director.
    B. Leadership, volunteers, program staff, and development staff.
    C. The CEO, the board, and an outside consultant.
    D. Program staff, the board, and an outside consultant.
    ANSWER: B

4. Which of the following has the best chance of success in a direct-mail program?
    A. Targeted mailing to a group of people who have a relationship to the organization.
    B. Targeted mailing to potential contributors who live in the service area and meet a certain income level.
    C. General mailing to prospects throughout the service area, both those who have and those who have not used the organization.
    D. Fundraising appeal to new residents in the service area.
    ANSWER: A

5. How often should you send direct mail to your donors?
    A. Twice per month.
    B. Once per month
    C. As many times as they respond.
    D. As often as they indicate they would like to receive mail.
    ANSWER: D

Domain 3: Relationship Building

1. Which aspect of an organization's history is MOST often effectively used in appealing to donors?
   A. The external factors that impacted the organization.
   B. The identity of the organization's chief executive officers.
   C. The inauguration of various departments or new services.
   D. The role of major donors in developing the current strengths of the organization.
   ANSWER: D

2. You have determined that donor retention should be a high priority moving forward. The BEST course of action to accomplish this is to:
   A. Recognise the donors publicly at events.
   B. Include the donors in upgrade efforts such as donor clubs.
   C. Invite new donors to contribute to other projects that need funds.
   D. Place the donors on the organization's mailing list.
   ANSWER: B

3. As a general rule, what is the best way to cultivate major gifts?
   A. Appoint prospective donors to the board.
   B. Organize a series of events for prospective donors.
   C. Develop informed repeat donors.
   D. Think like an investor while developing the request.
   ANSWER: C

4. When recognizing a major donor, it is most important for the fundraising professional to consider the:
   A. Donor's preference for recognition.
   B. Opportunities for publicity.
   C. Budget for high-quality recognition.
   D. Gift's significance to the organization
   ANSWER: A

5. Donors are most likely to not make a second gift when:
   A. They don't receive an annual gift summary to prepare their taxes.
   B. They are not thanked and informed about their gift's impact.
   C. They don't receive a thank you within 24 hours.
   D. They don't receive premiums with their gift.
   ANSWER: B

Domain 4: Volunteer Involvement

1. You have decided to include volunteers in the fundraising process. However, since this hasn't been a priority, there is no structure for this to take place. To set it up, you should:
   A. Select members from the existing board and start to recruit them.
   B. Ask for interested persons to volunteer, by publicising the need.
   C. Ask the CEO to identify people, and immediately recruit the CEO's selections.
   D. Take the time to identify potential volunteers for the organization, and then recruit them.
   ANSWER: A

2. Which of the following is the BEST volunteer recruitment source for a planned giving /bequest program?
   A. Clients and participants in past and current programs.
   B. Users of organizational services.
   C. Members, clients, and/or alumni.
   D. Board members, major donors, and financial professionals.
   ANSWER: D

3. To maximise the outcome of working with volunteer leadership, it is most important for the staff to:
   A. Obtain a list of likely prospects from volunteers.
   B. Prepare a detailed job description for volunteers.
   C. Provide for effective use of volunteer time and skills.
   D. Present a strong case for support using volunteers.
   ANSWER: B

4. How can volunteers be utilized to assess the giving potential of prospects?
   A. Ask volunteers to share their personal contacts.
   B. Ask volunteers to participate in the donor ranking process.
   C. Ask volunteers to make LinkedIn connections with high net worth colleagues.
   D. Ask volunteers to personally contact prospects and assess their giving capacity.
   ANSWER: B

5. What are the key elements of a successful volunteer retention program?
   A. Training, vision casting, and frequent communications.
   B. Fundraising training, regular emails, and frequent opportunities to volunteer.
   C. Clear expectations, training, timely thank you's, and regular communications.
   D. Clean and safe volunteer environment, food and drinks, and clear staff directions
   ANSWER: C

Domain 5: Leadership and Management

1. An analysis of the basic data (participants, income, and expenses) from a direct mail solicitation has been completed. To determine the key performance measurements and effectively evaluate the direct mail program, you will need to examine the:

    A. Percent participation, average gift size, net income, average cost per gift, cost of fundraising, and return.
    B. Hierarchy of gifts as compared to gift total, and gift total as compared to rated potential.
    C. Budget income projections as compared to actual income from the direct mail program.
    D. Performance of this year's direct mail donors as compared to last year's donors who did not give this year.
    ANSWER: A

2. Effective strategic planning for an organization must initially include:
    A. Hiring a consultant as the organization's planning process manager.
    B. Engaging key stakeholders in the planning process.
    C. Determining the organization's direction, mission, and vision.
    D. Conducting market research to assess potential opportunities.
    ANSWER: B

3. The most common reason for straying from an organization's mission is:
    A. Overemphasis on the bottom line.
    B. Changing community needs.
    C. Deterioration of leadership.
    D. Trying to do too many things at once.
    ANSWER: C

4. What metrics should be employed to measure the success of your fundraising efforts?
    A. Retention rate, giving frequency, and largest gift.
    B. Retention rate, average gift size, ROI, and percentage of goal achieved.
    C. ROI, cost per dollar raised, and percentage of goals achieved.
    D. Largest gift, smallest gift, and median gift.
    ANSWER: B

5. The elements of a successful fundraising plan include:
    A. A gift range chart, budget, organization chart, and dollar goal.
    B. Mission, goals, tactics, budget, and timeline.
    C. Goals, timeline, and budget
    D. Organizational chart, budget, and goals
    ANSWER: B

Domain 6: Ethics, Accountability, and Professionalism

1. What role does donor intent play in deciding how to use a gift of property?
    A. The donor is always right. Use the gift in the manner they prescribe.
    B. Donor intent should be balanced against the needs of the organization.
    C. Ultimately, the fact that it is a gift implies that the organization can decide how best to use the property.
    D. Donor intent should be honored as long as it does not violate your gift acceptance policy.
    ANSWER: D

2. How soon should donors be thanked for their gifts?
    A. Immediately upon receipt.
    B. Within 48 hours.
    C. Within 3-5 business days.
    D. All donors can be thanked on the 15th and 30th of the month.
    ANSWER: B

3. When visiting a senior donor in a nursing home, should a family member be present?
    A. If one is available, include a family member. If not, include staff.
    B. If the donor is mentally sound, a family member is not required.
    C. Yes, a family member should be present any time you visit a donor in a nursing home.
    D. If a gift is being discussed or agreed upon, then a family witness or power of attorney must be present.
    ANSWER: D

4. Should a gift be accepted from a corporation whose CEO is under indictment?
    A. No, it could embarrass the organization.
    B. If the property is not connected to the indictment and it does not violate the organization's gift acceptance policy, it is okay to accept the property.
    C. Yes. If it will help the organization, the source is not relevant.
    D. Yes, if the property can then be sold quickly.
    ANSWER: B

5. What should be included in a gift acceptance policy?
    A. Definition of acceptable gifts, recording and acknowledgement procedures, privacy procedures, and when to refuse a gift.
    B. Conflicts of interest, naming rights, and how to solicit matching gifts.
    C. Gift annuity rates, tax language, and donor research procedures.
    D. Stock transfer procedures, board member giving expectations, and employee giving enrollment.
    ANSWER: A

Appendix III

CFRE Accountability Standards

CFRE International serves the public by offering a certification program that recognizes fundraising professionals who are committed to the highest standards of ethical and professional practice in the philanthropic sector. CFRE International establishes and administers a voluntary certification process based on current and valid standards that measure competency in the practice of philanthropic fundraising.

Because CFRE International is responsible for ensuring the integrity of the credentials awarded, the Board has adopted a set of accountability standards related to the certification process. These standards exist to protect the public from those who would seek to misrepresent their qualifications or their status as credentialed practitioners. All individuals applying to, or certified by, CFRE International must comply with these standards.

It is likely that most professionals certified by CFRE International will belong to one or more professional associations that have codes of ethics related to the profession and the practice of fundraising. CFRE International's Accountability Standards, in contrast, focus solely on actions and principles related to certification and the certification process.

However, in those instances wherein:

1. an individual holding the CFRE credential is disciplined or sanctioned for violation of the Code of Ethics or Standards of Practice of his or her professional association, or
2. any organization involved in or connected to the profession, including regulatory agencies, takes action against the individual for reasons associated with professional misconduct, malfeasance, or unethical behavior

then CFRE International will consider taking action. CFRE International is most likely to take action when an individual's action clearly violates the integrity of the profession and/or universally accepted values and standards for the profession. In nearly all such instances, an individual who violates a code of ethics that was signed voluntarily has breached the CFRE core values of honesty and integrity.

Preamble

CFRE International, through the certification process, promotes the integrity and quality of the fundraising profession. CFRE International also endorses the Donor Bill of Rights and encourages all Certified Fund Raising Executives (CFREs) to do the same.

Accountability Standards (*This is the document you will agree by which to abide when you submit your application. Shown here for example.*)

As an applicant for certification or recertification from CFRE International, I submit that I subscribe to and am in compliance with the following accountability standards:

1. All information on my application for certification/recertification is accurate, truthful, and complete.
2. I will not make any claims regarding my certification status which are outside of the scope for which my certification has been granted, nor will I make statements concerning my certification status which are or which could be construed to be false or misleading. I will correct any such claims or misstatements immediately.
3. I will protect CFRE International's federal and/or international trademarks and use the CFRE designation only in the manner permitted by CFRE International. In addition, I will report to CFRE International any instances of misuse of the CFRE credential of which I become aware.
4. I will not transmit information regarding examination questions in any form at any time, nor will I accept or receive information regarding exam questions from any source other than CFRE International itself.
5. I will comply with all ethical and professional standards adopted by those professional organizations in which I hold membership.

Applicant Consent Statement

As an applicant for certification or recertification from CFRE International, I submit that I have read and understand the CFRE International Accountability Standards listed here and agree to be bound by them.

I understand that CFRE International reserves the right to verify any or all information on this application and that any incorrect or misleading information may constitute grounds for rejection of my application, revocation of my certification, or other disciplinary action. I authorize CFRE International, its officers, directors, employees, agents, and assigned examiners (the "designated parties") to review my application to determine whether I have met CFRE International's standards for certification. I agree to cooperate promptly and fully in any review of my certification by CFRE International, including submitting such documentation and information deemed necessary to confirm the information in my application. I indemnify and hold harmless CFRE International and its designated parties from the decision made on my application so long as such decision was made in good faith and does not constitute gross negligence by CFRE International or its designated parties.

I understand and agree that CFRE International may deny my eligibility to take the CFRE certification examination if any part of my application is incomplete or illegible, documented information does not meet the necessary point requirements, or the application does not include the correct fees.

I understand that I am to report to the testing location at least forty-five (45) minutes prior to the examination starting time. I understand and agree that I may not be permitted to enter the testing area if I arrive late for the examination and that I will not be granted additional time to complete the examination if I arrive late and am permitted to enter the testing area.

I acknowledge that I have read this application, Candidate Handbook, and CFRE International's certification standards, policies, and procedures. I understand and agree that if I am granted the CFRE credential, it will be my responsibility to remain in compliance with all CFRE International certification standards and requirements, as well as supply any information needed for the assessment. I understand that CFRE credential has a three-year certification cycle and that, if I wish to maintain my certification, it is my responsibility to maintain valid certification status by complying with all recertification requirements and submitting such proof of compliance as is required by CFRE International in a timely manner.

I understand that the information relating to the certification process may be used for statistical purposes and for evaluation of certification programs. I further understand that the information for certification records will be treated confidentially.

I understand that my violation of any of the CFRE International accountability standards or my noncompliance with any of the terms of this Applicant Consent Statement may subject me to disciplinary action by any professional association to which I belong and by CFRE International, including but not limited to the denial or revocation of my certification credential, and to possible legal action. I understand that, should my certification be withdrawn, suspended, or revoked, I must discontinue all claims to the certification and return my certificate to CFRE International. I understand that I may not use the certification in such a manner as to bring CFRE International into disrepute, and to not make any statement regarding the certification, which is considered misleading or unauthorized, nor may I use the certificate in a misleading manner. I also understand that if I act with behavior that is inconsistent with the integrity of the profession, I may be subject to disciplinary action by any professional association to which I belong and by CFRE International, including but not limited to revocation of my certification credential.

Endnotes

[1] CFRE International Dashboard, report to author, January 1, 2019.

[2] Association of Fundraising Professionals. *2018 Association of Fundraising Professionals Compensation and Benefits Survey.* (Arlington, VA: Association of Fundraising Professionals, 2018), https://afpglobal.org/sites/default/files/attachments/2018-09/2018AFPCompensationandBenefitsReport.pdf (accessed March 12, 2019).

[3] International Accreditation Forum. *The Value of Accredited Certification: Survey Report.* (Canberra City, ACT: International Accreditation Forum, 2012), https://www.iaf.nu/upFiles/The_value_of_accredited_certification_survey_report.pdf (accessed March 12, 2019).

[4] Marilyn Fischer, *Ethical Decision Making in Fund Raising*, New York, NY: Wiley, 2000, pp. 21.

[5] Fischer, *Ethical Decision Making in Fund Raising*, 21.

[6] Rouse, M. "What is Data Privacy," Techtarget.com http://searchcio.techtarget.com/definition/data-privacy-information-privacy. Accessed 22 November 2017.

[7] Demographics. *Dictionary.com* http://www.dictionary.com/browse/demographics. Accessed 22 November 2017.

[8] Katie Prine & Elisabeth Lesem, "Prospective Donor and Donor Research and Database Management," *Achieving Excellence in Fundraising*, 4th Edition, pp. 76-78.

[9] "Engage," *Dictionary.com*, http://www.dictionary.com/browse/engage. Accessed 11 November 2017.

[10] "Lifetime Value: What it Is & What it Isn't," FundraisingReportCard.com, https://fundraisingreportcard.com/donor-lifetime-value/. Accessed 8, October 2019

[11] Kent E. Dove, "Identifying, Researching, and Rating Individuals as Major Gift Prospects," *Conducting a Successful Fundraising Program,* Wiley, 2001, pp. 169.

[12] Kent E. Dove, "Identifying, Researching, and Rating Individuals as Major Gift Prospects," *Conducting a Successful Fundraising Program,* Kent E. Dove, Wiley, 2001, pp. 169.

[13] Kent E. Dove, "Identifying, Researching, and Rating Individuals as Major Gift Prospects," *Conducting a Successful Fundraising Program,* Kent E. Dove, Wiley, 2001, pp. 176.

[14] Kent E. Dove, "Tracing Philanthropy's Origins and Defining Fundraising Basics," *Conducting a Successful Development Services Program,* Kent E. Dove, Wiley, pp. 21.

[15] Kent E. Dove, "Defining Roles of Leaders and Top Volunteers in Fundraising," *Conducting a Successful Development Services Program,* Wiley, 2001, pp. 70.

[16] Kent E. Dove, "Recruiting, Educating and Motivating Volunteers," *Conducting a Successful Development Services Program,* Wiley, 2001, pp. 72.

[17] Kent E. Dove, "The Key Components of a Capital Campaign," *Conducting a Successful Capital Campaign,* Wiley, 2000, pp. 5.

[18] Dwight F. Burlingame & Sean Dunlavy, "Corporate Giving and Fundraising," *Achieving Excellence in Fundraising,* 4th Edition, 2016, pp.96.

[19] Dwight F. Burlingame & Sean Dunlavy, "Corporate Giving and Fundraising," *Achieving Excellence in Fundraising,* 4th Edition, 2016, pp.96.

[20] Timothy L. Seiler, "Developing and Articulating a Case for Support," *Achieving Excellence in Fundraising,* 4th Edition, pp. 41. 4th Edition

[21] "Endowment," *Investopedia* https://www.investopedia.com/terms/e/endowment.asp. Accessed December 1, 2017.

[22] Kent E. Dove, "Identifying, Researching and Rating Individuals as Major Gift Prospects," *Conducting a Successful Fundraising Program,* Wiley, 2001, pp. 159.

[23] Kent E. Dove "Identifying, Researching and Rating Individuals as Major Gift Prospects," *Conducting a Successful Fundraising Program,* Wiley, 2001, pp. 160.

[24] Roberta L. Donahue & Caitlin Deranek Stewart, "Special Events," *Achieving Excellence in Fundraising,* 4th Edition, pp. 417-419.

[25] "Trust," *Business Dictionary,* from http://www.businessdictionary.com/definition/trust.html. Accessed 1 December 2017.

[26] Kent E. Dove, "Identifying, Researching and Rating Individuals as Major Gift Prospects," *Conducting a Successful Fundraising Program,* Wiley, 2001, pp.160.

[27] Kent E. Dove, "The Key Components of a Capital Campaign," *Conducting a Successful Capital Campaign,* Jossey-Bass 2000, pp. 10.

[28] "Why America Gives", *Classy.com,* September 2018, https://go.classy.org/hubfs/_reports/why-america-gives/Why-America-Gives-Report.pdf (Why America Gives) pp. 6. Accessed 8 December 2018.

[29] "Why America Gives," *Classy.com,* September 2018, https://go.classy.org/hubfs/_reports/why-america-gives/Why-America-Gives-Report.pdf (Why America Gives) pp. 7. Accessed 8 December 2018.

[30] Margaret Rouse, "What is Data Privacy," *TechTarget.com,* May 2015 http://whatis.techtarget.com/definition/communication-plan. Accessed 1 December 2017.

[31] Patrick Rooney & Una Osili, "Understanding High Net Worth Donors," *Achieving Excellence in Fundraising,* 4th Edition pp. 194.

[32] Dwight F. Burlingame & Sean Dunlavy, "Corporate Giving and Fundraising, "*Achieving Excellence in Fundraising,* 4th Edition, Wiley, 2016, pp. 88.

[33] Dwight F. Burlingame & Sean Dunlavy, "Corporate Giving and Fundraising, "*Achieving Excellence in Fundraising,* 4th Edition, Wiley, 2016, pp. 90.

[34] "2018 Volunteering in America Report," *NationalService.gov* https://www.nationalservice.gov/newsroom/press-releases/2018/volunteering-us-hits-record-high-worth-167-billion. Accessed 8 October, 2019

[35] Renz, David O. *An Overview of Nonprofit Governance.* 2004, https://bloch.umkc.edu/mwcnl/programs-and-seminars/documents/an-overview-of-nonprofit-governance.pdf, Accessed 1 December 2017

[36] Tim Seiler, "Developing and Articulating a Case for Support" *Achieving Excellence in Fundraising,* 4th Edition, Wiley, 2016, pp. 43.

[37] Patrick Rooney & Una, Osili, "Understanding High Net Worth Donors," *Achieving Excellence in Fundraising,* 4th Edition, Wiley, 2016, pp.188.

[38] Eugene R. Tempel & Timothy L. Seiler, "Engaging the Board in Fundraising," *Achieving Excellence in Fundraising,* 4th Edition, Wiley, 2016, pp. 442.

[39] Eugene R. Tempel & Timothy L. Seiler, "Engaging the Board in Fundraising," *Achieving Excellence in Fundraising,* 4th Edition, Wiley, 2016, pp. 444.

[40] Kent E. Dove, "Defining Roles of Leaders and Top Volunteers in Fundraising," *Conducting A Successful Fundraising Program,* Jossey-Bass, 2001, pp. 64.

[41] Kent E. Dove, "Defining Roles of Leaders and Top Volunteers in Fundraising," *Conducting A Successful Fundraising Program,* Jossey-Bass, 2001, pp. 67.

42 Techopedia, "Data Integrity," https://www.techopedia.com/definition/811/data-integrity-databases. Accessed 1 December 2017.

43 Kent E. Dove, "Providing Accountability and Expressing Appreciation," *Conducting a Successful Fundraising Program*, Wiley, 2001, pp. 335.

44 Kent E. Dove, "Providing Accountability and Expressing Appreciation," *Conducting a Successful Fundraising Program*, Wiley, 2001, pp. 335.

45 Eric van Vulpen, "7 Human Resource Best Practices," *Digital HR Tech*, https://www.digitalhrtech.com/human-resource-best-practices/. Accessed 8 December 2018.

46 Derrick Feldmann & David Sternberg, "What to Do When Hiring A Consultant," *Philanthropy News Digest*, 7 July 2009. http://www.philanthropynewsdigest.org/columns/the-sustainable-nonprofit/what-to-do-when-hiring-a-consultant Accessed 8 December 2018.

47 "Accountability," *Merriam-Webster.com*, https://www.merriam-webster.com Accessed 10 November 2017.

48 "The Accountable Nonprofit Organization," *AFP.net Association of Fundraising Professionals*, 1995, (http://www.afpnet.org/Ethics/EnforcementDetail.cfm?ItemNumber=3262. Accessed 10 November 2017

49 Janice Gow Petty, *Ethical Fundraising*, Wiley, 2008, pp. 7.

50 "Gift Acceptance Policies," *Fundraising Fundamentals*, 2013 CASE (Council for Advancement and Support of Education), Section 10.6.

51 "Considerations in Negotiating and Drafting Gift Agreements," *Association of International Certified Professional Accountants* (https://www.aicpa.org/interestareas/notforprofit/resources/governancemanagement/considerations-in-drafting-gift-agreements.html. Accessed 11 November 2018.

52 Eugene R. Tempel & Timothy L. Seiler, "Stewardship and Accountability," *Achieving Excellence in Fundraising*, 4th Edition, Wiley, 2016, pp. 432-433.

53 Kent E. Dove, "Providing Accountability and Expressing Appreciation," *Conducting a Successful Fundraising Program*, Jossey-Bass, 2001, pp. 352.

54 Janice Gow Petty, *Ethical Fundraising*, Wiley, 2008, pp. 64.

55 Janice Gow Petty, *Ethical Fundraising*, Wiley, 2008, pp. 120.

56 "New Research Shows Concrete Benefits of Nonprofit Transparency," *Guidestar.org*, 8 January 2019, (https://learn.guidestar.org/news/news-releases/new-research-shows-concrete-benefits-of-nonprofit-transparency) Accessed 9 January 2019.

57 Marissa Luckie, "Building Windows in Philanthropy: 4 Benefits of a Culture of Transparency," *NPEngage*, 2 August 2018, (https://npengage.com/nonprofit-management/culture-of-transparency/) Accessed 10 November 2018.

Notes

Notes

Notes

www.ingramcontent.com/pod-product-compliance
Lightning Source LLC
Chambersburg PA
CBHW080215040426
42333CB00044B/2680